SELLING YOUR FILM WITHOUT SELLING YOUR SOUL

SELLING YOUR FILM
WITHOUT SELLING YOUR SOUL

presented by

prescreen

&

CASE STUDIES IN HYBRID, DIY & P2P INDEPENDENT DISTRIBUTION

BY THE FILM COLLABORATIVE, JON REISS & SHERI CANDLER

Selling Your Film Without Selling Your Soul
presented by Prescreen and Area23a:
Case Studies in Hybrid, DIY and P2P Independent Distribution

By The Film Collaborative (Orly Ravid & Jeffrey Winter),
Jon Reiss, Sheri Candler

Published by
The Film Collaborative
3405 Cazador Street
Los Angeles, CA 90065
www.thefilmcollaborative.org
All Rights Reserved.

Production Manager: David Averbach
Video Editor: Samuael Topiary
Trailer Editor: Gene Merker
Cover and Interior Design: David Averbach
Copyeditor: Susan Lynn
Camera: Jon Reiss, Jon Kendall Winter

Selling Your Film Without Selling Your Soul also is available in a digital version for all portable electronic devices. The digital editions include extra content such as video interviews with the filmmakers and instantly accessible URL links of examples and source material for a deeper understanding of the text found in this book.

ISBN:
978-0-9838229-0-5 [Apple iBooks Enhanced Edition]
978-0-9838229-1-2 [Apple iBooks Edition]
978-0-9838229-2-9 [Amazon Kindle Edition]
978-0-9838229-4-3 [Barnes & Noble Nook Edition]
978-0-9838229-6-7 [Barnes & Noble Nook Enhanced Edition]
978-0-9838229-5-0 [Paperback]

For bookstores and online wholesale sales contact:
SCB Distributors: +1 800-729-6423

www.sellingyourfilm.com

Table of Contents

Acknowledgments

The Film Collaborative (TFC) is grateful to Sheri and Jon for their delightful collaboration. Many thanks to all our sponsors for their support and to all our case study subjects for their diligent and transparent participation: Ari Gold, Anne Bernstein, Paul Thomas, Matt Harlock, Tom Gustafson, Casper Andreas, Javier Fuentes, Daniel Karslake, and Thomas Woodrow. Thanks to New Video for offering numbers for *Bass Ackwards*. Gravitas for their help with Casper Andreas' films and *American: The Bill Hicks Story*. Wolfe for their help with *Undertow* and *Were the World Mine*. Ted Hope for everything. David Averbach for over-delivering as usual. Gene Merker for rockin' it on the trailer front. Jon Kendall Winter for on-the-fly shooting. Samuel Topiary for video editing for the enhanced digital edition. Meredith Scott Lynn for the name of this book. To all the filmmakers and others who helped us narrow down the name. Susan Lynn for copyediting. TFC's Board of Directors and Board of Advisors for ongoing support. And special thanks to TFC legal counsel Cherie Song.

Jon Reiss would like to offer special thanks to Emy Takada, Rory Owen Delaney, Ted Hope, Hunter Weeks, Mike Dion, Ben Niles, Pat Weiser, Josh Shelov, Declan Baldwin, The IFP Filmmaker Labs, Lance Weiler, Saskia Wilson Brown, Jill Savarese, Gayon Augustine, John Gomez, Whitney Smith, Jonah and Cris Goodhart, my incredible collaborators Orly, Jeffrey, Sheri and of course my loving wife Jill Goldman and children Sam and Lucie Reiss.

Sheri Candler wishes to thank the following people for supporting her with time, love and patience while writing this book: my early "title testers" Nelson Carvajal, Richard Purves, Lucas McNelly, Chris Jones, Zahra Zomorrodian, Peter Ong Lim, Jeanne Bowerman, Obhi Chatterjee, Darren Young, and Dawn Mikkelson; Ross Pruden, Josh Bernhard, Bracey Smith, Nina Paley, Nicolás Alcalá, Jennifer Warren, Alberto Lopez, Cheryl Ingrassia, Cary and Kay Brown, Jason Brubaker, Rick Vaicius, and Phillip, Tristan, Juliana, Rick, Barbara and Erin who all think I'm mad but are willing to play along. Also my fellow collaborators Orly, Jeffrey, David, Gene and Jon who are all a source of support in many ways every day.

Foreword

by Ted Hope

Times _have_ changed for Indie Film. Yet Indie Film—as the public still perceives it—at first appears as if it hasn't changed with the times at all. Instead of truly evolving as a whole, Indie Film has come undone, and split apart. It has morphed into new forms, even though the publicity surrounding it still speaks as if everything were the same as people remember from back in the age of _Pulp Fiction._

What is this new world of Indie? Indie Film has bifurcated and fractured like the mass audience before it. Sure, some of its practitioners still spend significant budgets and lounge about at festivals looking for their knights to come rescue them. But clearly there are now the brave few, growing in number daily. These are the committed artists/entrepreneurs who have not only left the past behind, but are forging a new path that will herald a new era: an era which truly supports an ambitious and diverse creative culture, empowers both the creators and their audience, embraces the widest definition of cinema, and which accepts the responsibilities that come with it. This book that you now hold before you is _by and for those pioneers._

Selling Your Film Without Selling Your Soul proves that the dominant challenges of yesterday are now solve-able. Nothing is out of reach. The path to freedom has been found! We can throw out the old myth of maxing our parents' credit cards to complete a film only to sell it to a fat man for millions and millions. The pages of this book prove that "independence" is a true option now—at *every* step of the process.

How has Indie splintered, altered and changed, you ask? On one hand, "traditional" Indie Film remains; the kind that is brought out by the large-scale corporate entities. It may look and feel like Indie Film of old, but it is backed by a powerhouse of money. These films are released according to traditional "windows" and rarely return funds to the artists and their supporters who helped to make the film in the first place. On the other hand, we now have a Truly Free Film culture, which includes all the work outlined and studied in this book; work that was made free of the dreams of multi-million dollar corporate sponsorship and which benefits the audience *and* the artist, both financially and otherwise.

I have tremendous faith that our indie film culture and community will continue to improve—but that faith is conditional. My faith is ultimately in one thing and one thing only. My faith is in *people*, and by that I mean that I have faith that the individual filmmakers will reach out to the larger community. The generosity of those who contributed to *Selling Your Film Without Selling Your Soul*, by virtue of all the various artists' commitment to transparency, is close to awe-inspiring. "This is how it was done." "This is what we achieved." These are the statements that are made over and over again in thie book. It does not require a super human to achieve real success. It does not require having been born into or having bought your way into privilege. You don't even need to know anyone. What it does require is hard work and some know-how. The know-how is now in your hands. Only you can answer whether you can apply it and get it done.

The authors of *Selling Your Film Without Selling Your Soul* use case studies. They name names and cite figures. They tell you how it is done, when it is a success and even when it is not perceived as such. The sharing of our failures is something that historically the Indie Film Community has struggled with; breaking through that taboo of exposing our failures and limits is necessary if we are to establish a true entrepreneurial creative class.

I used to blame "The System" for the mainstream's lack of embrace of Indie Film. Lately I have recognized that the great barrier to progress is our *own* fault. The great barrier is the lack of transparency and that transparency begins with us. By definition, it is an openness to share not only our successes, but also our process and all that it entails. Until I read this book, I felt that the Indie Community had a lot of trouble committing to this openness. After reading *Selling Your Film Without Selling Your Soul,* I see a new transparency is before us.

We must invite and adopt true transparency. Both the practice of transparency and the examples the authors provide in this book are truly an inspiration. But beware! I couldn't help but take notes as I read it; with each chapter, my to-do list grew by several more points.

Sharing our failures is perhaps both the greatest need and greatest challenge of our new transparency. We learn more from our mistakes than from anything else, yet although we have all enjoyed the success of indie film in the past two decades, we have allowed our failures to vanish uncharted and unanalyzed. We cannot continue to allow this opportunity to grow escape us. The sustainability of our community and careers depends on it.

Change seems to be just one of the many constants of Indie Film. What seems revolutionary today will be ordained "best practices" next season. The amount of change we are all currently facing, however, is so great that at times it feels overwhelming. There is one way we can deal with this onslaught—and that is by sharing with each other, as a true community should and must. By providing us with the details of how others have not just weathered tsunani of change but triumphed over it, the authors of *Selling Your Film Without Selling Your Soul* are providing a new road map for others to follow. It is your guide to help you navigate the rocky landscape to the future.

Think about the world you want. Think about how you can now actually earn a living doing what you love. Think about how you get there and how you can sustain it. It is all more possible than ever before. I cannot imagine that such thoughts could lead you to any other process than one of sharing. Sharing leads to engagement—which then prompts action. Wonder why you aren't getting more done? Perhaps it is because you aren't sharing. This book has a wealth of transparency, with case study after case study prompting you to action. *Selling Your Film Without Selling Your Soul* shows how it is done, and what you can expect if all goes well. Don't break the chain! Don't do as others have done before you. Let's loosen up and build the ramps and bridges that can get us above the fray. Step out of the rain, and let the sunshine caress your forehead. It's a new day and you know how to get there.

Introduction

Dear Filmmakers,

We want for you what you want for yourselves, to have a sustainable filmmaking career, to find your audiences and connect with them, and to thrive creatively, professionally and financially.

Selling Your Film Without Selling Your Soul is the first of what we hope will be many in a series of case studies that highlight strategies and lessons from film releases that filmmakers can learn from, model after and hopefully even augment or expand on with their own films and releases. We're honored and thrilled to be collaborating with filmmaker/author/consultant Jon Reiss and social network marketing guru/strategist Sheri Candler. It has been a true pleasure collaborating with them and we treasure the ability to collaborate for the greater good, rather than compete for the lesser.

As the industry and business of film distribution and revenue streams changes in the face of new digital technology's impact on distribution and changes in audience and consumer access and habits, we collectively encourage _you_ to look at the source of success and then be liberated and empowered to discover that _you_ don't always need a line of gatekeepers or multiple middlemen to make your dreams come true. And even though there may be cases where to some extent the gatekeepers and middlemen make sense, it's almost never a useful paradigm on its own anymore.

The more filmmakers try to release films in a more hybrid or even fully DIY fashion, the less of a stigma some may feel about it and the more useful and appealing DIY will be, even as an attractive and comforting strategy to future investors and producers, as opposed to the present frequent thinking that privileges the all rights sale even with deleterious terms. DIY or hybrid distribution need not seem like a last resort. It need not seem less sexy. It need not seem less successful. It need not seem like a negative or blemish in any way. What filmmakers need is to access audiences and revenues from all sources, both for one's present work and one's future filmmaking.

The point and purpose of *Selling Your Film Without Selling Your Soul* is to highlight the questions filmmakers can ask, such as: "What is my audience?" "Where is it?" "Is a distributor more capable of reaching it or less so?" "Is there something an all rights distributor can do for my film that I cannot do myself?" and "If so, are the terms worth the difference?" The answers will vary but we believe asking the question(s) is key in every instance. This case study book highlights many of the methods and techniques and practices filmmakers can follow now and in the future to distribute one's work in the most filmmaker-friendly and sustainable way possible. There are lessons about what and who worked well and others not-so-much. The more filmmakers practice this the more powerful and useful and rewarding the filmmaker practice of this will be.

A NOTE ABOUT THE FIGURES IN THIS BOOK

We attempted to get at and publish every number and detail. We discovered that while we did do more than has been done before, we were nevertheless limited by corporate contracts that do not allow certain details to be disclosed. In those instances, we give indicators of the information, and the ballpark figures whenever possible. Even though we know them, some exact numbers just cannot be published. Other numbers that are sometimes omitted are the exact distributor fees. However, if the distributor's fees are in keeping with industry standard we note that, and if not we note that too. On the DVD side, industry standard is either taking a 25% or 30% fee (to the distributor) and recouping all expenses, or costs-off-the-top 50/50 (less common and costs must be capped always), or simply remitting 25% of gross receipts with no expenses recouped (and sometimes scaling up to 30% and 40% based on performance benchmarks). Fees in digital distribution are sometimes 15% (which we believe is a great #) and other times 20% or 25%…when it gets higher than that we believe there is something wrong. Of course the key is to know how many fees there are along the way and how the terms and practices vary between platform and distributor options.

WHY *THESE* CASES?

We each selected the case studies that interested us and served the overall parameters and goals of this book. We anticipate future editions that will even further expand the scope and diversity of the case studies.

SPONSORSHIP

With regard to sponsorship, we went after a wide range of folks that we felt ethically okay working with. The content came first and then the sponsorship, so there are times when sponsors are also referenced in the content and many other times when companies that are not sponsors are referenced in the content. No authored content in this book is paid for and nothing edited out because of relationships to companies.

ABOUT THE DIGITAL EDITIONS...

TFC acknowledges its Creative Director David Averbach's extraordinary talents and service both to this organization and to this project. We had originally conceived of this book as an interactive iPad App, but David convinced us that it was more in the spirit of this project to go truly DIY and self-publish, thereby sparing us a large developer fee (and possibly also a cut of the proceeds), streaming and encoding costs, not to mention a huge time delay to create an App. By choosing the ePub format, we sacrifice a bit of interactivity for the ability to offer the basic edition free of charge to filmmakers, and reach a wider audience at the same time. In response to certain requests, we have also added this printed edition.

A NOTE ABOUT TERMS

We realize that certain readers may not be familiar with the all the terms that are employed in this book. To this end, we are compiling a glossary of terms, which can be found on the *Selling Your Film* website (sellingyourfilm.com).

Many thanks to TFC Board of Advisor and supporter Ted Hope for his Foreword and immense leadership in independent film in general.

A big shout out to TFC Board of Advisor and dear friend, Writer/Director/Producer/Actor/Sizzle Reel Guru, Meredith Scott Lynn for coming up with our title, which we tested against many others via Survey Monkey, and it won!

We hope you enjoy this book, our first, of hopefully many more to come.

Sincerely,

The Film Collaborative
Filmmakers First.

About Prescreen

www.prescreen.com

[The co-authors offered the presenting sponsors of this book an opportunity to provide a more detailed explanation of how their services work.]

Prescreen is an online movie marketing and distribution platform that efficiently connects films to an audience they otherwise may not have the ability to reach. The goal of the Prescreen model is to create signal out of noise and present content in a way that makes it easy for people to discover new movies and share them with friends. Prescreen also serves as a tool for filmmakers and distributors to gain deeper insight into the demographics and behaviors of a film's audience for continued success.

Each day, Prescreen highlights one new movie by sending an email featuring the title to its list of opt-in subscribers. The movie's trailer is also featured on the Prescreen.com website for 24 hours. After being the daily feature, each movie continues to live on Prescreen for a total of 60 days. This allows the content owner to capture the resulting organic word-of-mouth marketing that ensues from being Prescreen's featured title. All titles are available to rent and stream on a pay-per-view basis.

Prescreen also leverages the social graph and encourages its community to use social tools, including Facebook and Twitter, to start and/or continue the conversation about each title. Users are incentivized to share movies with their friends, coworkers, and relatives to earn discounts and rewards. All featured titles will get a Prescreen Performance Report that includes detailed marketing information including key analytics, demographic information, and market research data for continued success.

Prescreen is only successful if your movie is successful. There are no out-of-pocket fees or expenses to be featured on Prescreen. All interests are aligned and revenues are shared between the content owner and Prescreen.

Visit prescreen.com to sign up to receive the daily deal or prescreen.com/submit to submit your film for consideration to be featured on Prescreen.

prescreen

About Area23a

www.area23a.com

[The co-authors offered the presenting sponsors of this book an opportunity to provide a more detailed explanation of how their services work.]

Area23a is an independently owned "event" based theatrical distribution company, co-founded by niche distribution specialist Richard Abramowitz and Ocule Films founder, Kirt Eftekhar. The company focuses on event driven films, providing value-added distribution through alternative ways of reaching audiences across the country, releasing films in convention and community centers, night clubs, casinos, libraries, museums, and college campuses, in addition to traditional venues like theaters, cinematheques and festivals. Area23a distributes award-winning films such as Dan Sturman and Bill Guttentag's SOUNDTRACK FOR A REVOLUTION, Michael Paul Stephenson's BEST WORST MOVIE, Alex Rotaru's THEY CAME TO PLAY, Gerardine Wurzburg's WRETCHES and JABBERERS, Gayle Ferraro's TO CATCH A DOLLAR, Adrian Grenier's TEENAGE PAPARAZZO as well as the upcoming REVENGE OF THE ELECTRIC CAR directed by Chris Paine.

Area 23a has an expertise in creating theatrical events, as well as traditional releases, that engage communities, featuring live panel discussions, post-screening parties and lectures. Whether distributing a nationwide theatrical event on 250 screens, a customized theatrical tour in over 100 cities or a single night "movievent," Area 23a connects our films and filmmakers to the local audience in each market by utilizing multiple marketing and promotional tools including but not limited to social media, street teams, non-profit and advocacy groups, city and state departments, corporate sponsors, and celebrity guests.

Through our extensive network of exhibitor and venue partners, Area 23a offers a unique "theatrical on demand" program that allows for filmmakers and audiences to set up "movievents" or theatrical engagements in virtually any market there is a demand.

Area 23a's distribution approach cultivates community, promotes dialogue and participation and will maintain a loyal audience base across all distribution platforms.

Bass Ackwards

by Jeffrey Winter

Bass Ackwards, *produced by Thomas Woodrow,*
directed by Linas Phillips

It was March 2009, and producer Thomas Woodrow had done everything right. He had produced his first feature, called *True Adolescents*, starring Mark Duplass and Melissa Leo, by first time director Craig Johnson. He had gotten into the SXSW Film Festival and, given the film's "indie grunge" feel, it was arguably the perfect festival at which to premiere the film. He had brought on a very well known, well-respected and accomplished sales agent in the form of Josh and Dan Braun of Submarine Entertainment. The premiere was packed, all the right distributors were in the room, and the film was good.

But then nothing happened.

Nothing—as in no offers from distributors, no sales of any kind. The film just kind of fell into that gaping maw of indie purgatory known to many—destined to travel from small film festival to small film festival without much rhyme or reason while the producers try to figure out what to do with it. I know, because I saw the film nearly a year and a half later as a juror for the Bend Film Festival, where we judged it the best film of the festival. Of course, awards from festivals like Bend don't really help a film find distribution. Fortunately for *True Adolescents*, the story ends better than most; now more than two years after the premiere *True Adolescents* is getting at a small platform theatrical release along with DVD and Video through New Video Group in the summer of 2011.

Flash forward a few months to the fall of 2009; Woodrow had completed a $35,000 micro-budget indie "road movie" called *Bass Ackwards,* by actor-director Linas Phillips (and executive produced by *True Adolescents* star Mark Duplass). Phillips had made a couple of docs before, but *Bass Ackwards* was his first narrative feature, (although its verité style and semi-autobiographical storyline incorporated aspects of his documentary background). Character-driven, leisurely paced, without any obvious marketing hooks and without any stars, the film is exactly the kind of contemporary indie that typically faces tremendous hurdles to distribution…unless it catches a "lucky" break. *Bass Ackwards* did catch that proverbial break. It was around Thanksgiving when producer Woodrow found out that the film had been selected for the 2010 Sundance Film Festival (January 21 – 31, 2010).

ABOUT THE FILM

From the 2010 Sundance Film Festival Catalog:

Yes, in Bass Ackwards a man drives a '76 Volkswagen van across America. No, the film isn't mired with the tired mechanics of a typical 'road movie.' This utterly original, lyrical, and visually exciting adventure has such a light touch that it quietly sneaks up and tugs you into an overpowering appreciation of being human.

When humble Linas, kicked off of his friend's couch and spurned by his lover, finds a forgotten van on a llama farm outside Seattle, he begins lurching east with nothing to lose. Slowly, the road eases him out of his relentless longing and into the moment. As his encounters with enigmatic characters take on subtly transcendent qualities, his shame and discomfort at being alone gradually give way to self-acceptance and connection. The dented, off-kilter vehicle, which valiantly, amazingly endures the journey, becomes a colorful metaphor for the human condition—our tenacity and hopefulness always tinged with imperfection.

—Caroline Libresco, Sundance Institute

Here's another description of the film—from the 2010 Seattle International Film Festival later that year—which further helps contextualize the film.

"In his first narrative feature, actor-director Linas Phillips takes his previous fascination with the films of Werner Herzog and embellishes them with touches of Linklater, Cassavetes, and his own low-key, quirky charm to create a unique and lyrical road movie. Kicked off of his friend's couch and reeling from a disastrous affair with a married woman, Phillips (the actor) decides to leave Seattle to return to his family home in Boston. Driving a neglected 1976 Volkswagen van he happened to "discover," he heads out of town—more to get away from things than towards something in particular. But Phillips (the director) knows that a road movie is always more about where the trip takes you

With *Bass Ackwards'* acceptance into Sundance, producer Woodrow had once again done everything right, and obviously the "logical" thing to do was to follow the same model he'd tried with *True Adolescents* by bringing aboard a respected sales agent and hoping for the best. Sundance is considered the "golden ticket" for U.S. indies; the best of all possible launches in North America for low-budget, character-driven films, but look carefully at its line-up every year–through the best years as well as the worst–and you'll find that many films get no distribution offers at Sundance. In fact, the vast majority of films don't leave Sundance with good distribution opportunities. Even those that do get distribution offers very often don't get the kind of offers that make a picture "whole"… meaning offers that are big enough to make back the budget of the film.

Of course there are spectacular exceptions every year, but Sundance is hardly a guarantee of distribution for films like *Bass Ackwards*. In fact, the film had been accepted into the newly created NEXT section of the festival, for low and no-budget films. Unlike the higher profile Premiere and Competition sections, the more "outré" sections like New Frontier, NEXT etc., are likely to be overlooked by traditional distributors who are pre-occupied with the flashier fare.

Given producer Woodrow's disappointing experience only

months earlier with *True Adolescents*, an idea began to take shape. Rather than trying to get traditional distributors to attend the Sundance screenings only to have them pass once again, Woodrow made the decision to take matters into his own hands and, as he puts it "flip everything on its ear this time."

> **Thomas Woodrow:** *We knew that the only one thing Sundance guaranteed us was a tremendous amount of publicity, a chance for people to hear about the film and to be curious about it. We also knew that we had an anti-commercial film, difficult to market, without an obvious target audience outside of the people that go to film festivals. We knew we had virtually no chance for traditional pick-up, and imagined that if we did things the regular way and waited for other companies to come to us, we'd probably see ourselves on IFC's digital platform six months later, and nothing else.*
>
> *We also knew that we had spent so little on the film that we could afford to take risks. So we decided to just go for the jugular and to use the publicity generated by Sundance to release the film directly to the audience. We knew we couldn't wait until people forgot about the Sundance press, so we decided the launch the film as wide as possible immediately after the Festival, meaning February 1st…one day after the festival concluded.*

Beginning around Thanksgiving, a unique and frenzied odyssey began. Woodrow teamed up with film marketer/publicist/distribution strategist Marian Koltai-Levine, formerly head of marketing at Fine Line Features and head of her own company, Zipline Entertainment, to develop a unique DIY strategy. (Note: Zipline Entertainment has since merged with famed Hollywood publicists PMK*BNC, where they have formed a marketing and distribution arm for the high-profile publicity firm.) The idea was relatively simple, but also relatively unheard of—to use Sundance as a publicity platform for releasing the picture directly into the marketplace; to subvert the system of *selling* one's film at a major festival and instead to use Sundance as a vehicle to go *directly* to the audience.

Woodrow started a Kickstarter campaign to help raise the funds needed to actually get the film to Sundance. Micro-budget indie aside, it still takes money to get the exhibition materials finished, book the travel and housing for the relevant cast and crew, get the necessary additional staffing in place and make sure all the i's are dotted and the t's are crossed. The Kickstarter campaign lobbied for $2,500, and the campaign actually raised more than twice that at $5,250. Apparently a lot of good will had already been generated by the film…always a very positive sign for a film launching into an extremely competitive marketplace.

However according to Woodrow, the actual cost for getting the film and the team ready and geared up for Sundance was closer to $15,000. This is a figure other filmmakers should consider carefully. $15,000 may be more than most filmmakers need to spend, but it should be remembered that the budget for delivery to film festivals, (which is generally not included in the average production budget), is likely to raise its ugly head just when most filmmakers are the least able to deal with it, i.e. right after the film is finished, the budget is exhausted and the credit cards are maxed out. That is usually the moment, when the chips are at their lowest, that the simplest financial decisions can make or break a film's chance at distribution.

I usually like to say that a film should put 10%-15% of its production budget aside for expenses linked to procuring distribution after the film is finished, recognizing that this is usually a luxury most films can't afford. Nevertheless, note here that *Bass Ackwards* incurred expenses for launching the film at Sundance that were far greater than my usual recommendation for percentage of budget…in fact, it was closer to 50%!

With Koltai-Levine working to book theatrical engagements to immediately follow Sundance, Woodrow took the extra step of ensuring the film was available as widely as possible and started working with one of the industry's top DVD and digital distributors, New Video. What they decided to do was unheard of at the time—to make the film available on major digital platforms (especially iTunes and Amazon VOD) *during* the Festival so that people could see it immediately upon hearing about it…and experience a Sundance film without actually having to be at Sundance.

Even more remarkably, New Video's DVD release was also scheduled to follow immediately after the Festival, with DVD pre-orders on Amazon.com set to go soon after the Sundance line-up was announced so that they could be shipped on February 1st.

In addition, New Video pushed hard to make the film available via Cable VOD on Comcast, Time Warner, Cablevision, and Insight Communications to go day-and-date with the February 1st release. However, given the enormous bureaucracy of the large cable carriers, the timeline ultimately proved too short to synchronize this window, and the VOD actually happened a month later (still extremely soon by most film release standards!). At its peak point, the *Bass Ackwards* Cable VOD release achieved penetration in 40 million homes

In other words, the entire strategy was conceived to make the film available to any consumer whose interest in the Sundance Film Festival would translate to watching a Sundance film, and to have *Bass Ackwards* be the film that was most readily available for them to see.

Here's how Woodrow described the release strategy of the Kickstarter campaign:

Woodrow: *This release is intended not only as a strategy*

> *to help Bass Ackwards gain attention and find its audience, but also as an open experiment in alternative distribution. In approaching Sundance as a platform rather than a marketplace, we are trying to pave the way, insofar as we are able, for a new era of filmmaker empowerment. We are not waiting around for someone else to tell us they want to distribute our movie. We know the movie's good. We're being proactive.*

Here's how Steve Savage, co-president of New Video, framed the release in a January 2010 press release.

> **New Video:** *The title, "Bass Ackwards," not only describes an offbeat and entertaining film, but also the spirit of the filmmakers who are joining us on this innovative ride. Together we'll be taking a film from its festival buzz immediately to an audience that is 'on the pulse' and wants to see it now. The digital age is an exciting time in the evolution of indie-film distribution with post-festival releases among the new paradigms.*

You can also watch Woodrow's description of the strategy used as part of the Kickstarter campaign on a video made at the end of 2009.

Now, anyone who has actually delivered a film to a distributor can well imagine how crazy the end of 2009 got for Woodrow and the *Bass Ackwards* team.

> **Woodrow :** *We had only found out that we got into Sundance around Thanksgiving, so suddenly we were faced with the fastest delivery schedule ever imagined. The idea was to have everything available at the same time as Sundance…so in addition to Sundance we had deliveries to iTunes, Amazon VOD, Playstation, etc., for during or immediately after the Festival. We wanted iTunes and Amazon to be available during Sundance, and Amazon, VOD and Playstation im-*

To complicate things further, the Sundance Film Festival chose 2010 as the year to launch a limited, non-exclusive 5-film distribution initiative with YouTube, which was the Festival sponsor of the NEXT section. A few weeks before the festival, Sundance and You-Tube announced that they were getting into the digital distribution rental business together…a major first for the Google-owned giant known previously for making content available for free. Sundance itself had dipped its toes into digital distribution back in the early 2000s, (making a selection of short films available for rental online during the Festival via its website), but had backed away from this initiative after a couple of years. The idea that viewers all over the world could pay $3.99 to watch five *feature* films *during* the Festival (three from 2010, two from 2009), seemed to be a potentially game-changing event, merging two of the best brands in the entertainment industry into a new way to monetize the delivery of independent films to audiences worldwide.

Bass Ackwards was one of the five films chosen—with the other four being 2009 award winner *The Cove*, 2009's *Children of Invention* and 2010 NEXT section titles, *Homewrecker* and *One Too Many Mornings*. The Industry buzzed with interest in the new partnership, both positive and negative, seeing it as a precursor to a new distribution model that could bypass the traditional distributor completely, albeit as a limited experiment in its initial stages.

For *Bass Ackwards*, the circle of publicity and buzz was now complete. With the indie industry mired deep in the recession, the message of what *Bass Ackwards* was doing was loud and clear. It was another harbinger of the DIY era…but with major industry veterans like Zipline and New Video along to help. With announcements of its novel distribution strategy, *Bass Ackwards* had already done what many small Sundance film aren't able to do… namely, rise above the "second-class" status of films in the smaller sections and make people talk about it. That was, of course, exactly the point of the strategy.

Of the buzz created by their tactics, perhaps noted journalist Eugene Hernandez in Indiewire said it best in a December 2009 article:

> **Eugene Hernandez:** *If you make, market, or simply care about the future of indie movies, keep an eye on Woodrow's approach. This is a first for a Sundance Film Festival movie. Will it be a defining moment for a new decade of film distribution and give emerging and established filmmakers new models to explore outside the system?*

For both *Bass Ackwards* and the Sundance Film Festival, the first evidence of how well the idea that Sundance "buzz" would translate into worldwide interest came back almost immediately from YouTube. On February 2, 2010 The New York Times reported that in the 10 days that the five films were available, there were a total of 2,684 views for total of $10,709.16.

Although several different media outlets reported slightly different numbers, (some suggesting the total number of views was actually lower), the closest thing to an actual breakdown of the titles by film was posted on slashfilm.com. during the Festival under a blog post heading entitled, "Analyst Declares Sundance's Youtube Streaming Initiative a Flop." Again, these numbers were posted during the Festival, so the final numbers would be somewhat higher. Nonetheless, this provided a good idea of the way the eyeballs on YouTube were being distributed.

film	*no. of rentals*
The Cove	303 rentals
Children of Invention	301 rentals
Bass Ackwards	299 rentals
Homewrecker	279 rentals
One Too Many Mornings	241 rentals

Keep in mind that *The Cove* had won the Sundance Audience Award a year earlier, played numerous festivals around the world to tremendous accolades, had been released theatrically to very good per-screen averages in the summer of 2009 (and would win an Oscar just a few weeks later), and yet the number of downloads was just barely above the others. Clearly none of the individual films were generating much attention, and the overall experiment of putting the films on YouTube that year just kind of…fizzled.

There was wide-spread Industry head-scratching and hand-wringing about why the YouTube experiment didn't perform and what it might mean for the future. In fact, most Industry people seemed to react to the numbers with glee, perhaps because very good results might have felt as if they were no longer needed, i.e. they'd be out of a job. (Obviously, successful direct festival-to-consumer distribution via digital platforms might spell the end of the Industry machinery as we know it).

The most popular opinion was that Sundance and YouTube just didn't market the experiment outside Industry circles. (YouTube apparently didn't even have a rental page that listed the films, according to published articles at the time.) It was also noted by most analysts that the community that regularly watched content on YouTube was not accustomed to paying for anything. There was such immediate and significant negative reaction to the move into the rental business from viewers that YouTube had to disable the ability to comment on the films' pages.

In addition, it was reported that it was exceedingly difficult to find the Sundance films on YouTube, a fact made humorously public when industry veterans Lance Weiler, Scilla Andreen, and Brian Newman blogged on SpringBoardMedia that during Sundance, the three had spent more than an *hour* at their Sundance condo trying to find the films to rent, with <u>*no success*</u>. (However, as I write this, I am happy to report it is now very easy to go to YouTube, type in *Bass Ackwards* and rent the film for $3.99. Thankfully, we've already come a long way since that (not so long ago) time.

Of course, what makes this *Bass Ackwards*/YouTube story compelling is that, as the first experiment of its kind, it set into motion the kind of inevitable, inexorable way that many film festivals are slowly moving into the distribution space – trying to capitalize on their brands as a way to help filmmakers as well as become distributors in their own right. Most notable has been the aggressive moves of the for-profit Tribeca Film Festival into both traditional and digital distribution spaces, particularly through its VOD channel its relationships with Comcast, Cablevision, Verizon FIOS and others, as well as via the Tribeca (ONLINE) Film Festival —an interactive, web-based film festival that occurs concurrently with the Film Festival. Nowadays, it is commonplace to be watching films via password-secured digital platforms like Vimeo, while its technology provider OpenFilm is working on new ways to leverage its film festival relationships into monetizeable film content online… but such was not the case in at the start of the 2010.

Given Woodrow's stated goal to go "as wide as possible" immediately after the Festival, a theatrical release strategy had to be in place. Keep in mind that because this was a micro-budget indie and he had made this decision just a couple of months before the release and wasn't interested in a traditional distributor, there was *no* P&A money in place—nor any time to raise it.

This is where Marian Koltai-Levine of Zipline Entertainment stepped up in a big way. Zipline was known as a fee-based, service-oriented distribution/marketing company—which traditionally means a company that puts out films for a monthly fee plus the P&A money–which is entirely the responsibility of the producers to raise and put toward the release. Instead, Koltai-Levine opted for an *equity* position in the film's release (exact % of equity undisclosed). They agreed to pitch theaters into going along with the novelty of what *Bass Ackwards* was doing, and to book the film on an opportunistic basis with theaters that could be sold on the idea—despite the lack of any P&A money to support the release.

It is important to consider the fact that most indie films today aren't actually looking to make money on their theatrical release, just to break even and generate reviews, publicity and buzz, but *Bass Ackwards* wasn't even counting on the theatrical for publicity. This was to be accomplished at Sundance. Just about every film gets some Industry trade reviews at Sundance, and *Bass Ackwards* was no exception. Reviews in *The Hollywood Reporter* and *Variety* were mixed, which is a risk every film takes when seeking to generate press coverage. They were, however, much better at *Huffington Post* and *Entertainment Weekly*.

Given the unconventional nature of the pitch to theaters (no traditional distributor, no P&A money, mixed reviews, no major awards etc.), *Bass Ackwards* was able to score what we generally call a "hybrid theatrical release," meaning bookings of a somewhat unconventional nature in independent theaters outside the biggest markets. Here's what it looked like…

dates played in 2010	city	venue
2/20	Lake Worth FL	Lake Worth Playhouse
2/20	Wilmington, DE	Theatre N at Nemours
2/27	Three Rivers, MI	The Riviera Theatre
3/11	Chester, CT	EO Art Lab
4/2–4/8	New Haven, CT	Criterion Theatre
4/2	Madison, WI	University of Wisconsin
4/9–4/15	Saco, MN	Cinemagic & IMAX
4/16	Portland, OR	Northwest Film Forum
4/16–4/22	Greely, CO	Kress Cinema Lounge
5/9	Ann Arbor, MI	Michigan Theatre
5/28	Portland, OR	Hollywood Theatre
5/29	Olympia, WA	The Capital Theater
6/10–6/16	Seattle, WA	Northwest Film Forum

While some might call this an "11 city release" in an effort to hype the theatrical presence, a quick look at these bookings makes at least one thing abundantly clear—none of the big independent theater chains in the major cities would show the film given the release strategy and lack of P&A (note: the major theater chains at the time were very publicly against day-and-date digital release strategies: happily, that has changed somewhat since that time). As a result, the film was not able to secure the kind of mainstream consumer publication reviews, (through such outlets as *The New York Times*), that most indie releases covet. In fact, *The New York Times* has a pretty strict policy that a film must open theatrically in New York plus at least a couple more major markets before it will review a film…which *Bass Ackwards* did not. Of course, New York is a famously expensive market in which to open theatrically, and this was not an option for the film.

The financial upshot of the theatrical bookings was, as producer Woodrow puts it, "negligible." (Exact theatrical figures are undisclosed and unreported.) According to my dictionary, the term "negligible" refers to "the quantities so small that they can be ignored when studying the larger effect." One could argue that theatrical releases for independent films are never "negligible," considering how the Industry instantly views films that have any kind of theatrical presence as different from films that are straight to DVD and digital. It was generally understood that *Bass Ackwards* was getting theatrical treatment, and that automatically increased the Industry buzz around the film. In addition, there was the extra marketing and word-of-mouth that any public presentations inherently generate. The film also played a few additional key film festivals, including the Seattle International Film Festival… although these festival bookings were limited, given the fact that the film was already available digitally at the time). From a filmmaker's point of view…these 11 "hybrid distribution" theatrical bookings would need to be considered a net positive, even if they didn't generate any real revenue.

For better or worse, very few independent films these days are looking to generate real revenue theatrically. It is the word-of-mouth, the reviews and the Industry presence that theatrical bookings generally supply that is wanted. Keep in mind that many indies every year pour significant money into theatrical releases, and often lose significant money by doing so. (I know, I've worked on a few of them.) In fact, "negligible" theatrical revenue is not something to overlook; for most films in the contemporary climate it is simply a *reality* to be grappled with—especially if the film spends absolutely no money on P&A or marketing materials!

Of course, as it was travelling through its hybrid theatrical, the film was also available on DVD (available to order on February 1, although the full retail push did not occur until June), as well as Cable VOD and key digital platforms like Netflix Watch Now, iTunes, and Hulu. The ultimate point of the strategy was to gamble on how the hype around the Festival and the unconventional release would drive these ancillary windows.

And so finally, we arrive at the all-important ancillaries.

As of 2nd quarter accounting statements from New Video in 2011, the gross receipts for DVD and digital platforms was $37,343.40. Breaking it down a little further, DVD units sold were a little under under 2,000, and the rest of the gross came from digital platforms. Note: Woodrow also carved out the rights to sell DVDs from the film's own website, but these sales were once again what Woodrow calls "negligible."

Of course, what is amazing about that number $37,343.40…is that its just about exactly what the film cost to make. And making back your budget is the basic gold standard of filmmaking.

With regards to how much of that actually got passed on to the filmmaker—Woodrow is not at liberty free to disclose the exact terms of his deal with New Video. However, the company is well known throughout the industry as being one of the most filmmaker-friendly distributors in the U.S. with respect to their splits with filmmakers. In general, filmmaker-friendly distribution splits range from 25%-50% for DVD, and 15%-50% for Digital… and New Video is acknowledged to be amongst the fairest/most favorable with its deals. According to Woodrow, "New Video was totally amazing throughout the process."

After factoring in distributor fees, one would also have to realize that there would have been replication fees, digital platform delivery expenses, etc. to be recouped. Therefore, if you do the fuzzy math based on the available figures above, it becomes pretty clear that the filmmaker would have made some five-figure money, but not enough to make back the initial budget of $35,000. (Also, Zipline's equity position comes into play here.)

Most importantly, this is a fact that Woodrow *readily acknowledges* in a positive way.

> **Woodrow:** *I have had the privilege of writing checks to investors within a year of the film's festival premiere. That is nothing to be sneezed at in this climate. In the end, I will not make my investors whole for the total amount of the production, finishing and distribution, but the film is truly out there and available. And people talk to me about it all the time, so it has had an impact and allowed all of us to continue building our careers which, against a relatively small spend, is a very real thing. And something is always better than nothing.*

Examined even more closely, *Bass Ackwards* emerges as a particularly interesting study of the difference between *Industry success*, and the *general consumer market*. As discussed at great length already, the film generated considerable recognition among so-called "Industry insiders"—which is extremely rare for a no-stars, no-niche, genre-blurring, character-driven indie. However, *Bass Ackwards* didn't necessarily take that step and convert that Industry buzz into general consumer awareness, a fact which Woodrow again readily acknowledges.

> **Woodrow:** *This really was an Industry play as opposed to anything that got noticed by a more mainstream audience. The intention was to create publicity buzz through the unconventional nature of the release and to have that alone drive audience interest in the film. It was definitely successful on that level. We did far, far better revenue-wise and exposure-wise than if we had tried to go a more conventional sales route, but in truth, Aunt Beatrice didn't download the film on iTunes in HD. It was an experiment, and within its own terms, I would call it a successful one. All involved learned an enormous amount about the machinery of marketing and distributing films, and the investors*

did get money back.

Again, as Woodrow puts it…"nothing to be sneezed at in this climate."

> **Woodrow:** *Of course, in hindsight it was also the nadir of the economy and the distribution picture, and things have gotten a little better since then," Woodrow concludes. "But really, how much better have they really gotten? So certainly I have no doubt we did the right thing for the times. What we probably really needed was more P&A money for distribution…if we could have raised $50K-$100K in P&A then I think it would have made a huge difference. In addition to the Sundance publicity, we probably needed the money to do some more traditional marketing and booking in NY, LA, and Chicago, and maybe some additional markets. That would have helped everything and probably made the difference making this into an unqualified success. So we built a car, but we didn't have enough gas for the car. It worked for the Industry…it was in fact, a "stunt" that the Industry talked a lot about and it really got the film 'out there' and helped our careers.*

In retrospect and from our outsider perspective, would the additional $50,000-$100,000 invoked by Woodrow have helped the bottom line? Maybe, but obviously we will never know. But where would that money have come from, and how would it have been possible given the overall strategy of going as wide as possible upon the Festival premiere? Would throwing $50,000-$100,000 toward a film that didn't cost that much to begin with and lacked marketing hooks even make sense?

To that I'd say that it is clear that if the filmmakers had decided they needed that money to release it into the market, then the timing would have been completely different, and that would have changed everything on the table (publicity, buzz, release schedule, etc.). To what effect, again, we will never know.

Was Woodrow's "experiment" with *Bass Ackwards* a success, or not? I leave that with you, the reader, to decide.

Feel free to let us know. Or better yet, let pioneering producer Thomas Woodrow know what you think about his films and his efforts…as I am sure that in today's digital reality you can find his online handles without much difficulty. It is almost as easy to find *Bass Ackwards* online and rent it—if only to help show Woodrow, Sundance, New Video, Zipline, YouTube, etc. that they were not completely off-base by trying to usher in the age when independent films are both available and monetizeable online.

Personally speaking, I congratulate the bravery and foolhardiness of all of them.

A New Path to Engage Film Audiences and Create Careers: An Introduction

by Jon Reiss

The three films that I researched for this book, while different in genre, size, year of release and experience level of the filmmakers also share a remarkable number of similarities in addition to their differences. I want to compare those similarities and contrast the differences in a structure that that I use to help filmmakers conceptualize strategies for their film's releases. Some of this system is included in my book Think Outside the Box Office, while some of it I have developed through my work with filmmakers over the past two years.

GOALS

It is essential to determine the goals of a particular project's release before employing any strategy for that launch. (Note—these goals are potentially different from those envisioned by the filmmakers when they set out to make their film.) In order to evaluate the success of a film's release, one must first identify the filmmakers' original objectives in releasing their film.

1. FORTUNE

Cold hard cash to pay back investors (and the filmmakers). This was the case with all three films. Each had investors that they needed to pay back, and this was a priority.

2. AUDIENCE

Having your film seen by the widest possible audience, (or any audience). In the cases of *The Best and the Brightest* and *Note by Note*, both film teams were taken aback by the lack of interest from the distribution community and were at a loss of how to respond. In different ways each sought to ensure that their film didn't languish, unseen, on the shelf like so many other movies. So, while recoupment was a primary goal, a second driving factor in their release strategy was to simply have the film viewed by an audience.

3. TRADITIONAL CAREER LAUNCH

In which the prestige of the release helps to get another movie made within the traditional studio or independent financing model. This was the goal of director Hunter Weeks for the release of *Ride the Divide* before he and producer Mike Dion realized that they each had different objectives. Eventually, Weeks agreed with Dion that the investors had to be paid back. Ultimately, though, through that recoupment process, Hunter was able to develop a new model of engagement for the film that led to his next project (see 5 below).

4. CHANGE THE WORLD

This is the desire of most documentary filmmakers (and some narrative filmmakers as well), and it became a secondary goal of *Ride the Divide*.

However, a fifth goal has emerged for filmmakers in the last few years which is much more achievable today than ever before:

5. A LONG TERM CONNECTION WITH A SUSTAINABLE FAN BASE

The goal here is different from number 3 in approach, attitude and technique. Instead of depending on other people (i.e. gate-keepers) to determine whether or not your film gets made, as is the case with the conventional studio career launch, according to the new model of filmmaking, it is your audience—and your relationship with your audience—that determines whether or not your movie gets made.

What I learned from the filmmakers of both *Note by Note* and *Ride the Divide* was that, although they started their releases with the initial goal of recoupment, in the end they realized that the hybrid strategy that they were employing to meet their objective created a relationship with a fan base that they could utilize and build upon for future projects. As a result, this has become a higher priority for both filmmaking teams as each pursues and crafts subsequent projects to capitalize on the audiences that they developed for the films that I am considering in this book.

AUDIENCE

My process of examining audience engagement for a film can be outlined in three questions/steps:

1. WHO IS YOUR AUDIENCE?

You must know your audience in order to have a chance of connecting your film with them. For most independent filmmakers, it is best if they can identify niche audiences to connect with, and to find a core within that niche. Each of the films in this section identified and engaged their core and niche audiences. For *Ride the Divide* it was bicycle enthusiasts and those who live along the Continental Divide. For *Note by Note* it was Steinway piano dealers (super-core), and music teachers (core). For *The Best and the Brightest* it was the super-fans of some of the film's stars (not the ones that you would expect), *and* the regular clientele who frequent the theaters that they booked.

2. HOW DOES YOUR AUDIENCE RECEIVE INFORMATION

How might you inform your audience about your film's existence so that they might be interested enough to watch it? Two successful avenues for independents have been organizational partnerships and social media.

Organizational Partnerships

Engage with organizations that share a common goal relevant to your film's niche, and who will connect you with their members. To do this effectively, you must determine how the relationship is win-win for both the organization and you. *Ride the Divide* is an excellent case of how filmmakers can create win-win partnerships with non-profit organizations *and* for-profit organizations (corporations and brand sponsorship).

Social Media

This involves a whole range of activity, from creating and cultivating an email list, establishing an engaging website and using social networks such as Facebook, Twitter and YouTube, to connecting with influencers, blogs and websites. Ardent fans of several of the actresses from *The Best and the Brightest* found the director, Josh Shelov, online. He engaged with those fans who subsequently championed the release of the film.

Essential to engaging social media is the 80/20 rule (perhaps it should be the 90/10 rule). This rule argues that only 20% of what you talk about in social media should be self-promotion (or promotion of your film). The other 80% or 90% should be information that is of value to your audience. If you only talk about yourself and your film, chances are that people will "un-follow you." An easy way to find content to talk about is to set up Google Alerts for topics/keywords that concern the world of your film.

3. HOW DOES YOUR AUDIENCE CONSUME FILMS?

Will they see it in a theater, buy DVDs, etc.? You should have a sense of how your audience consumes media in order to provide it in a manner that they desire. In their own way, all three films succeeded in (1) discovering how their audiences wanted to engage media, and (2) providing avenues for that engagement. Although *The Best and the Brightest* will have just started engaging ancillaries as this book is released, they are releasing all ancillaries simultaneously in order to best let the audience choose how they want to consume the film.

REDEFINITION OF FILM RIGHTS

I feel that the traditional way that film rights have been separated by the studios has been largely in reaction to technological developments. In other words, when television was invented, the studios created television divisions. When VHS tapes were invented, they created home video divisions. When the Internet arose they created digital divisions. However, while this system works well for the studios, the approach is not as helpful to independent filmmakers who are trying to figure out how to best achive their objectives. When considering the ways that an audience will consume a film, I think that the redefinition of film rights as laid out in *Think Outside the Box Office* is even more relevant today than when I wrote the book. In *Think Outside the Box Office*, I divided film rights into three basic categories: Live Event/Theatrical, Merchandise and Digital.

LIVE EVENT/THEATRICAL

In which the film is screened in front of an audience in the manner intended by the filmmaker. Any time, any place, and on any media. This redefinition enables filmmakers to claim the widest possible theatrical release. I would argue that a packed one-night screening is more valuable to the filmmaker and audience than a week of partially filled theaters. Why then is the week-long run considered "theatrical" and the one-night event is not? It makes no sense.

More important than "theatrical" is the notion of an "event." The event is something that the audience will perceive as unique, and special enough to motivate them to leave the house and devote their time to seeing the movie in a venue that the filmmaker/distributor has arranged for their viewing. The common consumer experience is a live communal event unavailable anywhere else.

Furthermore, what does the actual nature of the venue matter, so long as people are experiencing the film in a communal setting? No conventional theaters existed in the beginning of cinema; why accord them special status now?

The greatest similarity between the three films examined in this section is how they best exemplify this redefinition of "theatrical". Despite mainly booking conventional theaters via a traditional booker, *Note by Note* created unique events by showcasing the actual Steinway piano featured in the film, at many, if not most of the movie's opening nights across the country. *Ride the Divide* partnered with their soundtrack musicians (many of whom were selected for the film *because* they were based in their target location!) as well as local bike stores to create events catered to their audience.

The case of *The Best and the Brightest* illustrates the absolute need to redefine theatrical. According to every indicator except for traditional publicity, their "preview screening campaign" met with greater success than their conventional "theatrical" release: more people saw the film, the audience was more engaged (sold out screenings with stars appearing at one-night events), the film made more money and the filmmakers created a tremendous amount of grassroots awareness. Unfortunately, the traditional press still functions to primarily service traditional theatrical, so it was only when they booked the film into NY and LA, typically the most important cities in which to premiere a film (only 2 cities compared with 28 cities for the preview screening) that they secured mainstream film reviews as well as network television interviews for their stars. My fervent hope is that the growing success of live event/theatrical will persuade the traditional media that a film does not need to have a conventional theatrical release to be newsworthy.

MERCHANDISE

Merchandise concerns the sale of hard-good consumer products. For merchandise—the consumer experience is one of Object & Identity; I want that object because it has some intrinsic value and/or expresses something about me. If this purchase is driven by an underlying value of the object itself, then filmmakers would be wise to create and offer products with some fundamental value.

Note by Note did well with traditional DVDs. The jury is still out on *The Best and the Brightest*. *Ride the Divide* had a merchandise release as innovative as their live event/theatrical. Blurring the lines between events and merchandise, *Ride the Divide* created living-room screening kits that included the film and sponsored merchandise all in a nice wooden box. They also contributed half the proceeds to Livestrong, which they maintain greatly boosted their sales.

DIGITAL RIGHTS

Digital rights concern the consumption of a film when it has been delivered in the form of 0s and 1s. In *Think Outside the Box Office*, I detailed the minefield that the convergence of television/cable and broadband delivery was causing. For this reason I argued that it was important to combine these rights in the same category. However, I feel that there is another reason to put these rights in relationship to each other: they satisfy a common consumer experience: the need to watch the film "how I want it, where I want it, on the digital platform that I own." This is why New Video is going day-and-date with all ancillaries for *The Best and the Brightest*. *Note by Note* utilized an innovative approach to television, engaging PBS screenings, which boosted DVD sales and allowed the producer to sell underwriting time. So far, however, *Ride the Divide* has pursued the most innovative approach to their digital rights by coordinating their premiere on The Documentary Channel with both their iTunes debut and—most importantly—their free screening period on YouTube to launch their partnership with Livestrong.

I am constantly inspired by artists who create new paths to engage audiences and to sustain themselves financially. What follows is a look at three films that refused to take the traditional system's "no" for an answer. Instead, they struck out in unique ways to create an audience for their films and in the process discovered new methods to create and finance future projects.

Ride the Divide

By Jon Reiss

Ride the Divide, *produced by Mike Dion, directed by Hunter Weeks*

Ride the Divide is an inspiring journey about the world's toughest mountain-bike race, which traverses over 2700 miles along the Continental Divide in the Rocky Mountains. The film weaves the story of three characters' experiences with immense mountain beauty and small-town culture as they attempt to pedal from Banff, Canada to a small, dusty crossing on the Mexican border.

I met Hunter Weeks and Mike Dion at the Slamdance Filmmaker Summit in 2010 when they were on the verge of releasing their film into the world.

The two were hardly neophytes to the new world of distribution; Hunter previously self distributed 10 MPH and wrote a book about his experiences distributing that film. Because of their experience, they avoided falling into the trap of depending on film festivals to sell their film to a distributor that most likely would never come.

> **Hunter Weeks:** *You're ready to take the challenge on yourself and you're going to be successful because you're going to put way more work in than any typical distributor that comes together for your project, unless, of course, you're that 1% that is super extra-special.*

Matthew Lee in Southern Colorodo

GOALS

It was interesting that Hunter and Mike did not realize that they had conflicting goals for their release until I asked them what those goals were. Hunter wanted to launch another film (career),

Mike wanted to earn enough to repay the investors and perhaps turn a profit (money). (I suggest all teams get on the same page—it is vital to keep your release focused and on track!). They chose to go for the money. As a result of this focus, they have paid back their investor and garnered a lot of attention in the process, both of which will help Hunter launch his next project (although he "left a couple jobs on the table over the past year to focus on the release.")

MAKE YOUR FILM AS GOOD AS POSSIBLE

Hunter and Mike screened *Ride the Divide* repeatedly to make it as good as possible.

> **Hunter:** *That's the hardest thing when you're making your first film…cutting it down. You're going to cut and cut and cut. You're going to lose so much that you don't want to lose. You have to realize that you're so inside a project you really don't know what it looks like to people outside, but an audience teaches you that, and it's critical (to screen your film to audiences) before you go out and try to market something.*

AUDIENCE IDENTIFICATION

At Slamdance, we identified two main niche audiences to focus on: The first was bike enthusiasts. The super-core of this niche would be people who actually participate in the Tour de Divide race. The next layer (core) out would be mountain bike enthusiasts. The next layer (secondary audience) to reach out to would be devoted bike enthusiasts. The large outer tertiary layer of this audience would be people who live life to the fullest and embrace a positive lifestyle. As they left Slamdance, Hunter decided that they had to reach out to Lance Armstrong, because he was someone who exemplified this tertiary audience and was deeply connected to this niche. (More on this later.) Another related niche was people who are involved in endurance contests of one kind or another, but Hunter and Mike smartly decided to focus on bikers.

Matthew Lee deep in thought in New Mexico

The second niche audience we identified at the Summit was geographical: people who lived along the Continental Divide, e.g., the communities along the Rocky Mountains from Canada to Mexico. The core of this niche is the communities that live along the race route itself. A super-core would be bike enthusiasts who live along the Continental Divide. (It is totally fine to use two ways of looking at the audience to identify a core or super-core).

AUDIENCE ENGAGEMENT—PARTNERSHIPS

It was clear from the start that their niche audiences (especially the first one identified above) would be grouped into organizations, and it would make a lot of sense to partner with these groups to get the word out to their niche. This was tremendously successful for *Ride the Divide* as they engaged a two-prong strategy: (1)

National organizations for awareness and (2) local organizations to promote specific events and screenings.

> **Hunter:** *We have a couple of different classifications of partnerships. We have our corporate partners. Sometimes they donate money, sometimes they donate hard goods that we need, and sometimes they just commit to helping to bring exposure to the title. We worked with* Smartwool *on this film in a fairly big way. They came onboard with financial assistance to help us shoot this film. In turn, we would give them exposure and give their beanies to some of the riders, and if they happened to make it into the film that would be great. Then you have other types of partners, which are more oriented to the niche audience. In this case, that's cycling for us.*

> **Mike Dion:** Adventure Cycling Association *is a non-profit that actually designed the 'Great Divide' mountain bike route where the race and the film takes place. Once we hit the theatrical we worked with localized groups; for instance, when we were in Boulder we connected with the* Boulder Mountain Bike Alliance *that has a newsletter list of 7,000 people that helped market the film for that particular show.*

Their list of national organizations is impressive in addition to the ones mentioned: People for Bikes, Siren Bicycles, Spot, Ergon, Moots.

Note that Hunter and Mike approached working with these organizations with a win-win scenario in mind.

> **Hunter:** *With a partnership you have to look at what you're doing for that partner and how you're bringing visibility to what they do. Sometimes at our screenings we'd kick back a buck per ticket. We'd find little ways that made it beneficial to them to really partner with us.*

Ride the Divide also partnered with Livestrong. From September 22-October 2, 2010 they donated 50% of the proceeds from DVD, Blu-Ray and iTunes sales to Livestrong. This gives another incentive for the consumer to buy the film: it is not just a film, it is a cause. Note that they give 50% of the profits to Livestrong—not 5% or 10%. In addition, this generosity motivates the partners to help the film.

THE EXTRA BENEFITS OF DONATING TO CHARITY

I don't recommend that filmmakers work with charities in a purely mercenary way. As Hunter points out, you have to want to do good for the world and you want to be passionate about your charity.

> **Hunter:** *And, you have to be able to set aside the fact that you might not make the money back that you need to for your film. You have to be okay with that. But, when you do good, usually it comes back to you. In this case, the Livestrong community started to learn about the film and they helped support the screenings and buy some of our living room packages to raise additional funds for Livestrong. So, by working with a charity and helping to raise money for them, you're helping their audience understand what your film is about and what you're doing, and they start to give back to you in different ways.*

BE AUTHENTIC

When dealing with your audience, it is critical to be as authentic as possible.

> **Mike:** *If you're aligning with a charity or a non-profit you've got to be passionate about that particular thing. You can't just go do it because other people are doing it. Your audience is going to see through it, and it's going to seem fake and un-genuine. For me in particular, an inspiration of mine*

was a gentleman named Elden Nelson, otherwise known as the 'fat cyclist,' whose wife was affected by cancer and the Livestrong foundation really stepped up for him and really helped his family get through what they were going through. Elden has a blog called fatcyclist.com, which I was a big follower of, and he's got a pretty big audience. He inspired me to get back on a bike and start doing 100 mile races and inevitably step up and do what you know of as "ride the divide." With Elden as an inspiration for me, Livestrong just was a perfect tie, to kind of continue that movement. We've since worked with Elden and fatcyclist to raise money, and he's talking about the project in his inner circles, which has been fantastic.

Mike Dion on a snowy pass in Montana

SOCIAL MEDIA

Hunter and Mike started their social media push around the time of their world premiere at the Vail Film Festival, and since then "it has been a non-stop, almost daily process of engaging that audience. Moving forward, what that's done for us is that for the next product, that next adventure film, we've got that audience engaged."

Both Hunter and Mike feel that it is important not to barrage your audience with "me, me, me." On Facebook they asked cyclists to post photos of their bicycles and then picked the three best and gave them a digital download and a soundtrack.

> **Mike:** *I think that's effective engagement, and it's not just "this is the film and it's available at this price."*

TIMING

FESTIVAL LAUNCH

Hunter and Mike wanted the credibility that a film festival offers, so when they didn't get into Sundance or SXSW they decided to premiere at The Vail Film Festival, which made sense both because of their audience and because of their prior relationship with the event.

> **Hunter:** *We knew after that we wouldn't spend much time screening in film festivals, because quite honestly, we could build audiences just as easily and capitalize on the experiences versus letting the film festivals take all of the money from the shows that they screened.*

They started selling DVDs and conducting their live events one and a half months after their premiere at the Vail Film Festival.

PREMIERE DATE

If there are special days, weeks, months or seasons in which your audience is particularly primed to see your film, then you should take advantage of that. For *Ride the Divide* they knew they wanted to get the film out when cyclists were getting excited about riding again—in the spring.

> **Mike:** *I think it was imperative that we released the film in the spring, as cyclists are coming out of the winter doldrums and are eager to get back on a bike and experience that particular weather and that particular season, especially going into theatrical, because cyclists are used to getting together with their cycling buddies and their cycling clubs and gathering together and going for rides and beer. So that theatrical event tie-in, yeah, was absolutely perfect for the season we released.*

LIVE EVENTS

In keeping with their intelligent audience engagement strategy, Hunter and Mike wanted to utilize more components than a traditional theatrical release for their film; they wanted to incorporate all forms of public exhibition—traditional or not. To date, *Ride the Divide* has had 135 screening engagements! Hunter and Mike booked 25 of those screenings (all conventional theaters) and then their audience and the promoter who took the film and booked engagements for them handled the rest. (See breakdown below.) In my book, that's a 135 city theatrical release.

> **Mike:** *Pretty much everything we did was in a conventional theater, more of an indie-type theater. Definitely, we weren't hitting the AMCs or anything like that, but we were able to put together, probably 90% of the theaters we did. We worked out a 50/50 split, which took any risk off us. We broke it up into legs, so we would put together a Denver-Salt Lake City-Boise-Portland-Seattle sort of show, that would take us on the road for 9 or 10 days. Then we would come back and do some business work and some more marketing. I think to be out there for a full 40 or 50 days is tough, it's difficult, it's going to wear you down, and it's taking you*

Mike and Hunter are working on a 40 city tour with their new film, *The Path*, but this time their main sponsor is doing PR/marketing and stepping up as a true partner in the release.

Here is some of what they found:

THE PARTNERSHIPS PAID OFF

For them it was key to have national organizations to promote awareness, but also, more importantly, to have the support of local groups and commercial entities (bike shops, etc.). In Dallas, TX for instance, Villy Customs brought bikes to the screenings to enhance the experience. They also had bike valets at several locations. This type of grassroots support ensured the local screenings of *Ride the Divide* were always well-attended.

Hunter Weeks, director, on a sat phone, during production

CREATE AN EVENT

As much as they could, Hunter and Mike created a sense of an event around their film. In addition to bike themed events, they also enlisted musicians. One of the bigger risks they took was to *four wall* (in which a filmmaker rents the "four walls" of the theater) their premiere at the Boulder Theater (which wouldn't give them a percentage deal), for their opening night on May 22, 2010. I'm not usually in favor of four walls for most films, but at times it can make sense and even turn a profit. Hunter and Mike were nervous about pulling the trigger on this event because of the nut ($4,500), but they realized that this was the best-case scenario for their premiere—Boulder being not only a Rocky Mountain community, but also a strong bike community.

Hunter and Mike made the premiere a premium event by providing a film and musical experience, including a performance by Gregory Alan Isakov, who also appears on the film's soundtrack. It paid off for them. They charged $18 per ticket and with 600 people in attendance, they grossed $10,800 in one night. They paid $3,000 to rent the theater plus $1,500 for the musician fees and other costs. That's a $6300 theatrical profit for one night (not including the sweat equity to arrange and market the show). They did other event screenings with another *Ride the Divide* soundtrack musician, Dominique Fraissard.

PROGRAM ON ALTERNATIVE NIGHTS

Echoing the experience of Todd Sklar and his Range Life tours, Hunter and Mike found that the best nights to screen were Wednesday and Thursday, with Monday and Tuesday being fine as well. Most of their screenings were 1-3 nights, except in Denver where the film ran for 3 weeks. They strongly recommend staying away from Friday and Saturday nights because there is too much competition and Sundays "are the worst." Note: Saturdays did work well for bike-event themed screenings when a group ride or bike shop got behind the screening.

AUDIENCE HOSTED SCREENINGS

For their audience hosted screenings, they had a 2 pronged strategy:

Initially they charged $295 for screening licenses that included the DVD or Blu-ray, posters, postcards—a screening pack. Through this they grossed about $25,000 selling 37 through their online store, 7 through email and phone, and over 50 via an avid evangelist who ended up becoming a promoter of the film, paying a reduced licensing fee and setting up his own shows. This promoter also split sales of DVDs at the show 50/50 with producers.

Then they created a wonderful wooden box screening kit for $99, of which 50% of the proceeds went to Livestrong. The box not only contained the DVD, but a T-shirt by Mighty Karma, a Smartwool Beanie, a book by Tony Hsieh and Livestrong bands and stickers. Note the win-win partner relationship. Other sponsors donated products, which made the package more valuable. They credit fatcyclist.com's promotion of the boxes as key to their success. In addition, not only did the filmmakers provide a value, they provided scarcity, numbering the boxes and limiting them to 500. They have sold 200 of these packages so far, raising $6500 for Livestrong (and $6500 for themselves). So far they have donated $14,000 to Livestrong through the release of the film.

All together, they figure they have netted $43,000 from their theatrical release.

In Hollywood terms, it's not *Avatar*, but in independent terms it is a huge win to make a decent profit on theatrical while engaging partners and creating awareness for the film.

Help us support LIVE**STRONG** and be a part of Ride the Divide's national launch on the Documentary Channel or celebrate LIVE**STRONG** Day with friends and an inspiring movie. **Get a group together in your living-room on 9/22 though 10/2** to watch the movie either on the Documentary Channel or on DVD/Bluray and help raise money for LIVE**STRONG**. The movie is inspiring people to live life to the fulest, which is consistent with Livestrong's (and our partners') missions.

The package is $99 with **50% of proceeds benefitting Livestrong.** ONLY 500 PACKAGES WILL BE SOLD.

Included in the package is:

- A DVD or Bluray
- A custom wood laser-engraved box by karvt.com
- A limited edition t-shirt by Mighty karma
- A SmartWool Beanie
- Tony Hsieh's Best Selling book — *Delivering Happiness*
- Other sponsors goodies
- Two Livestrong bands
- A free iTunes download of 10 MPH, the director's first feature film
- Documenatry Channel bumper sticker
- Over $125 in value

Ride the Divide created living-room screening kits that included the film and sponsored merchandise all in a nice wooden box

MERCHANDISE

Hunter and Mike began selling DVDs at their live events. They started selling from their online store in April just after their world premiere at the Vail Film Festival (DVD, Blu-ray, Poster, Soundtrack). They've sold 2,500 DVDs and Blu-Rays through their store. To date they have grossed $72,000 from all merchandise in the on-line store (this includes around $13,000 for the screening boxes).

TIMING PART 2: SELLING DVDS DURING THE THEATRICAL

It is pretty common practice now for films taking a DIY route to sell their DVDs at their theatrical. However, a number of films have started holding back their DVDs to encourage community screenings. The *Ride the Divide* team felt that it was important for them to sell DVDs as early in their release as possible to capitalize on the publicity from the live events.

> **Hunter:** *We noticed that DVD sales would increase in the regions we were screening in. We sold a considerable number of DVDs on our website. I think you're doing yourself a disservice if you're doing a theatrical and you get a big PR, or someone picks up your story and the community knows about it, and then the public can't act on it by being able to purchase a DVD on a website.*

But they are not just selling from their online store—they partnered with Video Action Sports and Rep Net, who buy them at between 40% and 50% of the retail price for each DVD sold—about $10.00 per DVD. They researched each of these wholesalers to make sure they were 1) getting a good deal that made financial sense and 2) that the wholesalers had good reputations for paying independent filmmakers. These distributors get the *Ride the Divide* DVDs into larger chains and into major on-line retailers. They've sold 1,800 DVDs & Blu-rays through their wholesale accounts— grossing approximately $18,000. Note: Video Action Sports paid on time up until a few months ago and are now behind about 5 months on some of their purchase orders.

They then repurposed their Living Room box for Christmas packages as high quality bundles for consumers who like to spend more to get more.

SOUNDTRACK

It is a common conception that "film soundtracks don't sell," but I believe that you need to consider each film individually. In the case of *Ride the Divide*, they specifically targeted bands that lived in one of their niche communities. They used a source for music called SonicBids.com, where musicians offer their music for use in films, events and concerts. Half of the musicians in RTD came from Sonicbids and they specifically searched for musicians from the states along the Rocky Mountains.

They happened to place an artist from the Red Pill label who was interested in releasing a soundtrack and doing the work to create it. Another win-win partnership was born, with the record label promoting the album that promoted the film, a technique that the studios have been employing for years. This opens up the film to a whole other audience: the indie music world. RTD bought the soundtrack from the label for $5 and then sold it retail for $14. The label also puts it on iTunes, which creates another level of awareness for the film.

RTD gets a small cut of the digital downloads as well, but again, they are not so concerned with monetizing every aspect of the soundtrack as they are with the added audience reach it provides.

It also helps with their future relationships with musicians.

> **Hunter:** *One of the hardest challenges with an independent film is how to pay for the music. By having produced a soundtrack that favors independent musicians and gives them more revenue, it helps us for future projects. We can talk to musicians and show them ways we're trying to be helpful to them—that we find ways to give them money whether or not the film makes money.*

A NOTE ON FULFILLMENT

To keep costs down and profits high the *Ride the Divide* team uses E Junkie for a shopping cart and fulfills their merchandise orders themselves.

> **Mike:** *In addition to just selling a DVD and a Blu-ray, we were selling bundles, posters and things like that: it can become really expensive to have a fulfillment house start fulfilling things that are non-traditional.*

DIGITAL

Mike and Hunter pre-sold their US cable rights to the Documentary Channel in order to have the funds to finish the film. Contractually they can't disclose the exact amount of the deal, but they were able to say that it was mid-five figures, which was higher than normal because it was a co-production deal. They aired the film on September 22, 2010. Note the smart timing—they began their tour well in advance of this date. They were already selling DVDs well before this "free screening" on cable, and then were able to benefit from a potential cable/TV bump of sales. Even though they used the September 22nd airing as the official launch of the DVD, they had been shipping since June.

Mary Metcalf-Collier in New Mexico

The film went on iTunes day-and-date with the screening on the Documentary Channel. However, they didn't publicize this, preferring to wait and take advantage of the Livestrong promo discussed below. They were featured on the documentary page. New Video is handling their conventional digital rights and probably helped them garner that placement. They are now on iTunes in US, Canada, UK, Australia and New Zealand. *Ride the Divide* reached #23 recently in the documentary category in the US and has been in the top 50 for quite a few months. They've done over 500 purchases and 2000 rentals in the US.

They also sell iTunes compatible downloads from their website, but "iTunes is 700%-800% better than what we're doing on our own website." It is good to use conventional channels when possible; people like to buy things where they are used to buying things. Hunter and Mike also noted that the digital download is a favorite of people in foreign countries, who don't want to wait for or pay for shipping.

They then scheduled the rest of their digital rights within a close proximity to the airing of a 2711 minute free access to their film on YouTube to coincide with Livestrong Day. At the end of this promotion on YouTube, they had just over 157,000 views.

They "turned on" YouTube rentals after that (due to the amount of traffic still coming from all the embedded trailers for the free YouTube screening). They've had a total of 200,000 views so far (they are unsure how many are paid rentals).

Note how they used a limited YouTube free screening to create a sense of an on-line event. They timed this event to coincide with an event of one of their key partners to help create awareness and to launch the digital component of their release, providing another bump in the media landscape. They found that the YouTube event did not generate as many DVD sales (only 50 over the 2 day period) as they were hoping for. However, they believe that they will make several thousand dollars from their YouTube partnership participation (ad revenue share), and contend that their YouTube presence has increased their overall sales of the film on various platforms through the fall. In a sense they considered the YouTube screening their "national release." They don't think that they would do this type of free Internet screening at the beginning of future releases, but they feel that they are effective for creating bumps later in a release.

Finally, for digital they signed an agreement with Babelgum to license a 10-part episodic series of the film in 7 countries. This was distributed online and via mobile devices.

THE FUTURE: GOAL NUMBER 5—CREATING A SUSTAINABLE RELATIONSHIP WITH LONG TERM FAN BASE

While Hunter and Mike's initial goal was to recoup their investor's money (and Hunter's goal was to get publicity to launch his career) they discovered that by doing the distribution themselves, they succeeded in achieving a much more powerful goal: connection to a fan base that could sustain their artistic careers.

PART 1— KEEP PROVIDING THEM PRODUCT

Because the race that they filmed is an annual event, Hunter and Mike plan on returning to film more footage this year. They then will release a two disc updated DVD to provide on-going products for their audience.

> **Hunter:** *That's the exciting part, in this independent film world you can keep it going and keep exciting people with what you have.*

They also plan to keep their sponsor integration going by creating exclusive clips to further product integration where its "natural and makes sense."

PART 2—THINK OF THE LARGER NICHE

Through their work with Livestrong as well as engaging their audience, Hunter and Mike realized that their true wider audience was "people that want to live life to the fullest each day." This includes a broad range of people centered in outdoor activities, endurance contests etc.

> **Mike:** *Now that we have* Ride the Divide *out there, for future projects we now have the audience and the lists so that we can engage them from the start.*

IN SUMMARY—KEY TAKEAWAYS

There are a number of takeaways that Hunter and Mike have from their experience.

1. Pay attention to who your audience is—and integrate that understanding into your release.
2. Tailor an event based strategy to work with that core audience and motivate them to come to screenings.
3. Work with partner organizations to reach your audience.
4. Do deals with people you want to work with down the line—create long-term relationships for a long-term career.
5. Understand that the audience you are developing is more general than the specific core you started with. This was huge for Hunter. His film was not just about a bike race—but was about "people who were embracing a positive life style—living life in a rich way." He was able to reach elements of this broader audience starting with his core—and this is the audience that he wants to make films for in the future.

Mary Metcalf-Collier riding in the New Mexican desert

Note by Note

By Jon Reiss

Note by Note, *a film by Ben Niles*

Note by Note: The Making of Steinway LI037 (hereafter *Note by Note*) is a feature-length independent documentary that follows the creation of a Steinway concert grand, #L1037. The film spans 12 months from forest floor to concert hall and features 12,000 parts, 450 craftsmen and countless hours of fine-tuned labor in Queens, NY. The film was produced, directed and distributed by first time feature filmmaker Ben Niles.

FESTIVALS AND PREMIERE

Note by Note had its festival premiere at the Hamptons Film Festival in 2006, and Ben presumed as do most filmmakers that he would be able to use a prominent festival like the Hamptons to sell his film to a distributor. He was able to obtain a top sales agent, Cinetic Media, to sell his film. Steinway brought the actual L1037 piano to the festival and arranged for a pianist to play at the premiere (more on this later), and Niles thought that the buzz and excitement at the event would help land him a deal.

However, that proved not to be the case. In the first year of *Note by Note*'s festival launch no sale was made.

> **Ben Niles:** *We didn't make the deadline for Sundance and we didn't get into Toronto or Berlin, so I think that really took the wind out of Cinetic's sails. I don't think they really felt like they had an opportunity to create that bidding war. So I'm sitting in my office wondering, what's going on?*

Cinetic told Niles that they "are not in the business of putting you in the festivals; we're in the business of selling your film."

> **Ben:** *Well, all these festivals are going by and I haven't sent the film in. I'm missing great festivals and they said, "Well, that's your responsibility."*

(In fairness to Cinetic—no sales agent can (or will) handle the daunting task of submitting a film to every relevant festival—in fact it is a huge job for individual filmmakers to take on with the plethora of festivals that exist, even with the existence of Withoutabox.com)

> **Ben:** *I remember that day. I immediately got on the web and started trying to figure out which festivals were about to close and I was submitting to everything because I just felt like my film was about to die. We didn't have that Sundance*

Ben's lawyer informed him that he had a clause in his contract with Cinetic that allowed him to get out of the agreement if no sales were made within the first year. (My experience with Cinetic is the same—they don't want to hold rights from filmmakers if they cannot help the filmmaker monetize those rights—they are very filmmaker-friendly in this regard.) When Ben amicably parted ways with Cinetic they supplied him with a spreadsheet listing everyone who had seen the film, and what their notes were. Both Film Forum and PBS had expressed interest. Ben contacted the Film Forum where Karen Cooper was a big fan and that became their premiere.

Ben: *We did two weeks, we had great crowds; we got press in every New York magazine, newspaper, television and radio station. I mean that blew it out. We were lucky because two films per month get their in-house publicist and we didn't have to spend a penny on publicity.*

This premiere was in November of 2007, nearly a year after their premiere at the Hamptons festival.

AUDIENCE ENGAGEMENT

AUDIENCE IDENTIFICATION

The team started with the core: Steinway owners and pianists who played Steinway pianos, then moved on to all pianists, music teachers and musicians.

Another audience group they discovered comprised people who worked with wood such as boat builders and carpenters.

Workers in the Steinway factory

Ben: *When we screened in Vermont I had all these people come up to me and say, 'You know, I have a business; I make furniture and I loved watching these guys build this piano.' It really gets down into doing things by hand, so I think anybody who likes to grow organic tomatoes or cook in the kitchen, or anybody who's really doing something tangible can really identify with the film.*

PARTNERSHIP/SOCIAL MEDIA

When Ben didn't make a sale, he realized that besides distribution, audience engagement also became his responsibility. He hired a distribution consultant, Peter Broderick, who told him to make his website more engaging and to start collecting email addresses at festivals. He added music and film clips to the site.

Ben: *When you click from page to page you can hear dif-*

ferent pieces of music and we put all kinds of information about the tracks in the film. I actually never did blog. At the time I was really playing catch-up and frankly, I just had too many balls in the air.

Ben was ultimately able to amass an email list of 6,000 people through DVD sales and people from festivals or theatrical screenings.

STEINWAY DEALERS

To keep the film authentic and impartial, Ben had kept an arms-length relationship with the Steinway organization, even though he was filming in their factory. He didn't want to give the impression that the film was a promo for Steinway. However, his lawyer indicated that he needed to get an agreement with them in order to be able to release the film, so he cut a 10-minute excerpt and showed it to the company executives. They loved the project, and at Ben's request gave him a letter of support to show to potential financiers. Additionally, they signed a contract permitting him to use the location footage as well as the Steinway name.

When Ben finished the film Steinway offered to show it at their dealer meeting.

Ben: *I didn't even know they had a dealer meeting, but of course I was happy to do it. Once we screened the film for the dealers, that really unleashed a wonderful resource for finding new fans of the film because every dealer in that room, and there were hundreds, said "When can I get my hands on this film? How can we help you promote it?" I was nervous about that, because I didn't set out to make a film to promote the Steinway Company or promote a Steinway piano. I fell in love with the story for many different reasons. But if* Note by Note *can help sell a few more pianos, I'm happy. The craftsmen deserve it.*

Piano bodies at the Steinway factory

OTHER ORGANIZATIONS

Ben also did a lot of outreach to music organizations, schools and teachers. He took out ads in a few trade publications for music teachers, and eventually hooked up with an organization that had 25,000 member teachers. Before the organization would promote the film Ben needed to produce lesson plans to sell with the DVDs. He eventually found a professional lesson plan writer. Ben said, "I didn't know that people do this for a living." The organization then blasted it to its whole email list and Ben offered discounts for a number of months.

LIVE EVENT/THEATRICAL

THEATRICAL BOOKER

> **Ben:** *I was trying to find an indie distributor and I was getting pretty frustrated because these people that I was told were indie distributors still wanted me to spend $50,000 to $75,000. They wanted me to get a 35mm print; they wanted a ton of money for P and A, and I said, "I guess I'm missing it, because that's not indie to me."*

Ben met with Jim Brown from Argot Pictures and they agreed on a monthly fee for Jim to book the film theatrically. The successful Film Forum screening was crucial, because theaters across the US look to NY box office figures to see what might be good to book locally.

> **Ben:** *Jim and I worked out a guaranteed three-month deal to see if he could get any traction for the film, and then we would step back and renegotiate if everybody was happy. Well, we renegotiated like within six weeks. The phone was ringing off the hook.*

Within the first year, they had 50 theatrical and 20 alternative theatrical dates grossing $100,000.

ALTERNATIVE THEATRICAL

Argo charged $250 per screening against 35% of the door for alternative theatrical screenings. In addition, Ben charges $1,000 for appearances, plus travel and expenses, and he keeps any revenue from post-screening DVD sales. Alternative theatrical has brought in about 40% of the $137,771 overall screening revenue, or about $55,000 of all theatrical revenue.

THEATRICAL EXPENSES

Since the New York theatrical was done at Film Forum, who provided the publicist, Ben was able to keep the costs of the theatrical release very low. He spent a total of $4,500 on publicists in LA, SF and Chicago, which Ben thought was very effective and a wise spend. He also spent $3,000 on print ads, (which Ben considered a waste of money), and $500 on dubs.

EVENTS

One aspect of *Note by Note* that I personally love is the live events, which feature the actual piano in the film. Steinway offered to move the piano to quite a number of their screenings, and the local dealers arranged for a local pianist to play at those events. To date, Steinway has participated in 30 of the 70 total screenings.

> **Ben:** *The theaters were happy, and then the dealers were happy that they could kind of cross pollinate, and they're still doing that. I mean, now that they were on PBS, if it's gonna air in Phoenix next month, then they get in touch with the PBS affiliate and they try to do a private screening.*

(More on PBS later.)

MERCHANDISE—DVDS

Ben sold DVDs at the screening, although Film Forum did specify a holdback on the DVD sales.

> **Ben:** *They cut us a little bit of slack because they knew that we needed to do it.* [Basically what they said to the theaters was,] *the director is going to be there, the piano is going to be there; all they want to do is say that if people want to buy the DVD—they can do that in the lobby.*

About 30% of the theatrical audience was converted to DVD

buyers—around 30-40 DVDs per night—which at $20 a DVD comes to $800 per screening—a nice bit of added revenue—especially considering the theater generally does not take a commission on these sales.

> **Ben:** *Some people would buy six, and say "I'm gonna give 'em out for Christmas gifts."*

An astonishing 5,200 DVDs have been sold from the website grossing $124,000. Unfortunately Ben fell victim to the demise of the fulfillment company Neoflix, who still owes him $6,000. In addition, Ben was eventually able to land New Video as a DVD distributor for the film. New Video was able to sell 3,000 units to Netflix as well as additional sales to brick and mortar stores and their on-line equivalents. The gross from New Video is $133,247 in a year and a half, of which Ben has netted $80,127. New Video gets 25% of gross DVD sales and 15% of digital sales for a 5-year deal.

EDUCATIONAL SALES

The music teachers, who were buying DVDs with the lesson plans, bought home-use DVDs.

> **Ben:** [I figured the teachers] *are not institutions and it was more important for me to just have the DVD in their hands because they're exposing it to other people.*

There are different rates for libraries, elementary schools and universities, and even though most can buy the DVD as home use, some actually do pay at the higher educational rate.

DIGITAL

TELEVISION/PBS

From the Cinetic spread sheet Ben knew that PBS was interested in the film, but only an hour long version. As is normally the case, it was up to Ben to pay for that new edit. You need this edit for most documentary foreign television sales.

PBS did not offer to pay for the television rights to the film. Their position was that since they were going to carry the film via common carriage and it would be covered by every affiliate in the country, giving the film massive exposure in their mind, they should not have to pay for the film. In essence, PBS feels that they are giving free advertising space (and Ben says that their sales continue to spike after these airings). However, PBS will give two minutes of underwriting time that the filmmaker can sell to sponsors.

> **Ben:** *I think its value is certainly in the six figures for the four 15 second spots that they give you. The problem for us was that the economy was tanking. I mean we tried everything; we even hired a guy who does this for a living. We had conversations with AMEX and we had conversations with Coca-Cola, but nobody was able to do it. There was nothing I could do about the economy tanking, but I tried to do this by myself for about eight months* [before he brought on the specialist], *and I would never let a friend do that. There's a small, small community of agents that do this specifically for PBS broadcast. We could have seriously made some big money there and sadly it just wasn't in the cards.*

CONVENTIONAL DIGITAL

Gross digital revenue to date is $15,000.

INTERNATIONAL

Films Transit took on the international sales of the film, charging a 30% sales fee with expenses capped at $3,000 (this expense cap is exceptionally low). They have grossed $20,126 in foreign sales with deals in Greece, Germany, Canada, France, Brazil, Finland, Al Jazeera (the Arabic-language network) and about five other smaller markets.

LONG-TERM CAREER DEVELOPMENT

Ben is currently working on a new film titled *Some Kind of Spark,* which follows inner-city kids taking weekend music classes at the Juilliard School in New York City. He is being much more aggressive with social media this time around, (which he didn't do at all for *Note by Note).* Even though the film is still in production, there is a Facebook page and a website. Ben will start blogging soon.

A major factor in audience development was Ben's Kickstarter campaign for *Some Kind of Spark*, which he utilized to generate money as well as audience awareness. Kickstarter raised $20,000 from 200 backers from seven different countries.

> **Ben:** [The 6,000 emails that were cultivated from *Note by Note* have been] *really instrumental in helping fund this project. It's hard to calculate exactly how many people from my email list contributed. I will say that at least 75% of the people who donated to this new campaign were more or less strangers to me. They were not close friends; they weren't names that I recognized immediately. A lot of people that did donate bought* Note by Note *or saw it somewhere and made a point of saying that they would make the donation. In fact, I heard from a person who saw it at IDFA in Amsterdam, who was apparently on vacation and got back after the campaign and said "Oh, I just saw your e-mail and I saw* Note by Note *a few years back and I want to support*

you." It's nice to hear from those people, but it's nice to know that we're also reaching people that are new to Note by Note *or this new project.*

LESSONS LEARNED

There are some things that Ben will do differently in his current and future projects based on his experience with *Note by Note:*

- Start the audience engagement process earlier (as just noted—he is doing this already).

- Get help.

   Ben: *I'm trying to find more help where I can. Having interns available to do stuff for me so that I can do more creative work. I'm much more open to delegating. There are just too many things to take care of. I'd love to actually start another project while this one is a year along. It's more important to me now to create a body of work than to just hold on to every little aspect of a film.*

- Partner with organizations.

   Ben: *I'm much more aggressive about finding organizations that could benefit from seeing my film(s) made. For instance, with* Some Kind of Spark *we are approaching music education and music related programs to partner with. We can help spread their agenda via our resources while we gain awareness, and hopefully funding, through their resources and social media channels. The right fit is a win-win for everyone involved.*

The Best and the Brightest

By Jon Reiss

The Best and the Brightest, *directed by Josh Shelov*

The Best and the Brightest (hereafter "*Best*") is a modern-day farce in the vein of *Tootsie* and *A Fish Called Wanda*. Set in the world of New York City's elite private kindergartens, *Best* centers on a fresh-faced young couple from Delaware, Jeff (Neil Patrick Harris) and Samantha (Bonnie Somerville), who have only recently moved into town. The comedy focuses on the extreme lengths they must go to in order to get their five-year-old daughter into school. The film was produced by Patricia Weiser, Robert Weiser and Nicholas Simon and directed and co-written by Josh Shelov.

I had the pleasure of meeting co-producer Declan Baldwin

at the IFP Filmmaker Labs in NYC, where I am one of the year-round mentors. Baldwin presented an intriguing method in which he garnered 200 sold-out screenings in a 28-city live event/theatrical release of a film that had not gotten into any "major" film festivals. Baldwin agreed to be interviewed for this book and subsequently introduced me to producer, Pat Weiser, who also agreed to be interviewed.

Weiser, along with her producing partner and husband, Robert Weiser, had prior experience with the documentary Bigger, Stronger, Faster. However, the Weisers still felt uncomfortable selling all the rights to the film to another entity, since they were unsure whether or not they would see any backend. At the time, though, they didn't see any viable alternative to the conventional method of releasing independent films—e.g., it was the "way it's done."

> **Pat Weiser:** *We were disappointed with* Magnolia. *Through* Bigger, Stronger Faster *we learned how Hollywood distribution works; that whatever you get up front is all you're going to get, and no one will make a real commitment to your film other than you. It was an expensive lesson. At the end of the day I think Magnolia just bought BSF to add to its library, with no real intention of marketing the theatrical or DVD/VOD/digital releases. Notwithstanding the balance sheets I've seen, it is tough to imagine they spent what they claim they did.*

The Weisers intended to use a hybrid model for their next movie, but that film turned out to be *Best,* starring Neil Patrick Harris, Amy Sedaris, John Hodgman, Bonnie Somerville, Kate Mulgrew and Bridget Regan. Because its budget was $3.7 million, Weiser felt that she needed to sell the film to a distributor in order to repay her investors.

Sneak Preview Press Coverage
Photo courtesy of Victoria Souza Photography

GOALS

Although a strong goal of Weiser's is to "figure out a distribution model that works for indie film," her primary goal is to repay her investors. She told me that "One of the primary indicators of 'success' from everything we've done will be the amount of profits we earn at the end of the day. That's the only thing that's going to allow me, as a producer, to do this again." She's not sure "which goal is more ambitious!"

TRYING TO SELL THE FILM

They finished the film in between late 2009 and early 2010, but they did not get into the Sundance, Toronto or Tribeca film festivals. According to Baldwin, the team started to take the lack of prominent festival interest personally, despite understanding that the movie wasn't a typical festival film.

They engaged a sales rep and held distributor screenings in NY and Los Angeles in March 2010. Weiser: "All the acquisition execs were howling during the screening—but when they went back to their sales team they were told 'we can't sell that.'" Weiser found out that the mini-majors "can only spend money on what they can sell to everyone"—e.g., a mass audience.

They turned down a number of six-figure all-rights deals because, as Weiser stated, "that would not make them whole and they would never see a back end."

According to Baldwin, for about 6-7 months the investors and filmmaker were a bit shell-shocked. The Weisers had intended to use the Pennsylvania tax credit of $700,000 as the funding for distribution and marketing (an idea I proposed to filmmakers in *Think Outside the Box Office*). The investors got nervous about the lack of sales interest and wanted to be paid back from the tax credit. In addition, no one felt that the cost of the proposed service deals (e.g., paying a distributor to take the film out theatrically) were worth the money. These service deal offers were for $150,000-$350,000 for a very modest release. Weiser said, "If I write a check—I want to know what that will get us."

In the fall of 2010 they resigned themselves to take one of the low money DVD deals that they had been offered initially, and in February of 2011, they signed with New Video because:

1. They were the most excited about the film.
2. They had a reputation for having very transparent accounting.
3. They had a very good experience releasing Neil Patrick Harris' Dr. Horrible's Sing-Along Blog.

At around the same time, they decided to arrange some screenings. In Baldwin's words, "We wanted to see the film in the manner that it was intended to be seen."[1] Since the director Josh Shelov attended Yale University, they were able to set up a "Yale in Hollywood" screening along with a few others. The reaction was overwhelming, and "shocked them into action," according to Baldwin. In essence, they realized that their film was good. The fact that they didn't sell it as they had hoped indicated that it was the market—not the movie—that was the problem. This brought up the question: how to tackle the market.

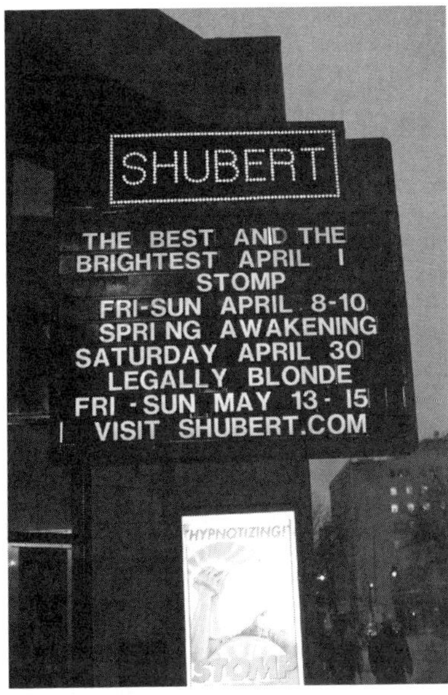

The Shubert Theater Sneak Preview
Photo courtesy of Victoria Souza Photography

PREVIEW SCREENINGS

Weiser and Shelov approached Baldwin to see if he would expand on the success of these one-off screenings to make the title

---

1   I emphasize this because I feel that this is one of the prime reasons that live event/theatrical screenings are still important.

more recognizable. The LLC for the film gave Baldwin non-exclusive semi-theatrical rights to the film (e.g. in one- or two-night runs in traditional and non-traditional theaters in the US with admission charged). They started off by four-walling a couple of theaters in NYC (Landmark's Sunshine Cinema in Manhattan, the Bell House in Brooklyn), New Haven and Phoenixville.

They wanted these screenings to be events—both by virtue of the one-time screening and by having the cast and crew appear. Amy Sedaris agreed to come to the Sunshine Theater in Manhattan. John Hodgman agreed to go to the Bell Theater in Brooklyn. Bridget Regan, Bonnie Somerville and Kate Mulgrew attended the Cinefamily screening in Los Angeles.

Post Screening Q&A at the Sunshine in NYC:
L-R Amy Dotson from IFP, Amy Sedaris,
director and co-writer Josh Shelov, co-writer Michael Jaeger
Photo courtesy of Victoria Souza Photography

Post Screening Q&A with Josh Shelov

Because of the success of these screenings (sold out, netting a few thousand dollars), they expanded the process. They created a low-budget office in NY and created a BluRay master. The New York staff (all of whom worked for nothing or peanuts) included Erin Miller, Corey Deckler, Mark Oxman and Jill Savarese. Each of these people had contacted the film and said that they wanted to participate in some way. Savarese became in charge of publicity; another was in charge of determining which were the best theaters to get involved; and another coordinated the local street teams. Weiser sent Baldwin $5,000 to help support the staff, while the rest was bankrolled by Baldwin and paid back through the screening revenue.

After the initial success, they booked into another 5-6 theaters. When some of the cast appeared at a screening, Savarese was able to get local television coverage for the events in smaller markets.

Packed house at a Preview Screening
Photo courtesy of Victoria Souza Photography

PARTNERING WITH YOUR AUDIENCE

One of the unique aspects to *Best*'s release was how Baldwin and his team created a network of local marketing partners across the US.

Baldwin realized early on that they needed someone on the ground in the local markets—essentially an advance marketing team—to distribute postcards, posters and network with friends and family. As a result, Baldwin's team would post on Facebook and Craigslist in the local markets to find these advance volunteers, and there was always a response. Baldwin discovered that there are "bright, motivated people across the US who want to connect with filmmakers outside of their regular jobs." It also helped that Shelov had been actively engaging with fans online; most of the people who came on board had already interacted with the director. Baldwin noted that this connection and engagement was essential to making this system work.

Bridget Regan and Neil Patrick Harris in
The Best and the Brightest

Shelov notes that it is not the big stars that drove this activity:

Josh Shelov: *Once we started directly engaging with our fans on Facebook and Twitter, we realized that many of our most active fans weren't necessarily the fans of our bigger names; they were fans of Bridget Regan and they were absolutely insane with passion. These are the fans who have reached out to us directly, rallied their communities, and quite literally dragged the film on their backs into their local movie theaters. Kate Mulgrew's fans have done the same thing. There's a worldwide group of hugely passionate, social-media-loving female sci-fi fans. The* Neil Patrick Harris fans *may be our greatest in number, but the* Bridget Regan fans, Kate Mulgrew fans, John Hodgman fans, *and* Peter Serafinowcz fans *have been the greatest in actual activity, promoting the film to their networks, creating fan posters and fan art, and actually taking to the streets to ask their local theatres to book the film.*

Kate Mulgrew in The Best and the Brightest

Here is a chart of the stars' social-media footprints. Note that this is about engagement, *not* numbers.

	Twitter	*Facebook*
Neil Patrick Harris	1,624,662	215,154
Bonnie Somerville	1,131	224
Amy Sedaris	not on twitter	54,437
Peter Serafinowicz	584,022	2,395
Christopher McDonald	not on twitter	551
Jenna Stern	1,211	24
Kate Mulgrew	2,141	10,698
Bridget Regan	20,359	16,357
John Hodgman	592,495	5,591
The Best and The Brightest	1,120	1,937

the stars' social-media footprints

Shelov also announced an online poster competition for the film—a woman in the UK ending up winning—and they printed and used her poster design for the preview screening release.

The winning entry in the film's online poster competition.

In just two months, by the end of April 2011, they had already had 50 screenings in 15 cities.

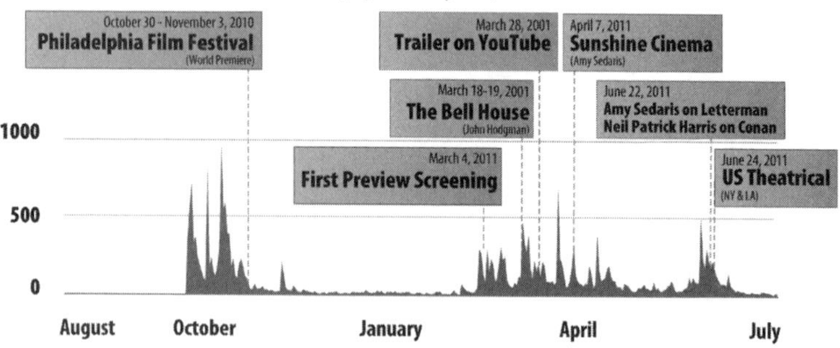

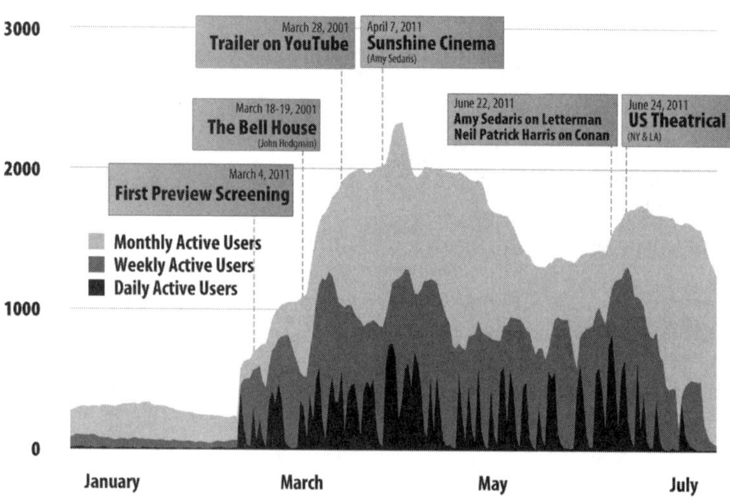

THE IMPORTANCE OF CURATORSHIP AND AUDIENCE CONNECTION

Baldwin felt that they had worked out a system bypassing traditional media buys. Outside of some Facebook ads, a few small banner ads and some local event listings, they did not spend any money on media buys. Hence, they felt they could book into an indie theater, do a great grassroots campaign, and thcy would sell out.

However, they discovered that this was not *the* formula. In Columbus, OH and Houston, TX they booked into well-respected independent theaters and had local teams marketing the film. In Columbus the theater was across the street from a university; it was the main art-house in town with multiple theaters. In Houston they had more "demand it" requests than in any other city. However, both of these cities bombed surprisingly.

From this Baldwin learned that the advance team helped, the online social media helped, but what was essential was that the theater needed to be connected to its own audience. To that end, they had the most consistent success with membership-oriented theaters whose patrons trusted the curatorial taste of the theater.

> **Weiser:** *Traditional theatrical is not connecting with audiences. What Declan did made sense because each of the theaters we booked into has a connection with their audience.*

These audiences trusted "their" theater—and if the theater programmed it—they would come.

Their webmaster was Brian Chirls, known for his groundbreaking work on *Four Eyed Monsters* (Chirls now runs a company, Crowd Controls, that helps filmmakers create demand tools for their websites). A surprising note on *Best*'s Demand-It tool on their site: Baldwin found that there was no correlation between the number of people who "demanded" a screening in their city and box-office (as exemplified by the Houston screening). However, the surprise benefit of the Demand-It tool was that it was a good source for local marketing volunteers. Baldwin successfully reached out to the people who had requested a screening in their town and persuaded them to be the local outreach people for those screenings:

DEMAND A SCREENING NEAR YOU

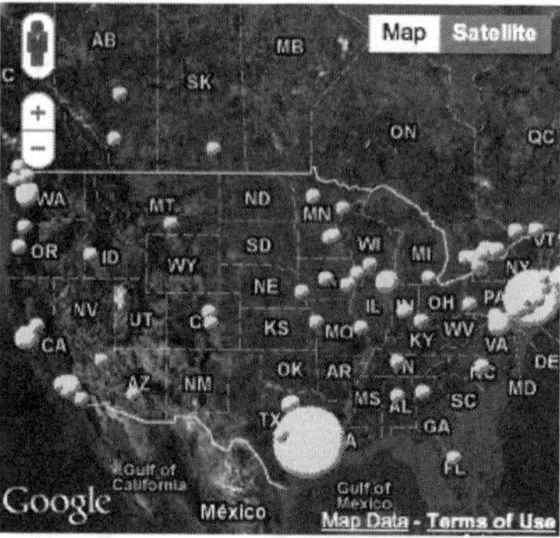

Demand-It tool on home page of
The Best and the Brightest *website*

After Houston and Columbus, they were much more selective about the theaters that they booked. They had to be member-oriented theaters. To this point, their success allowed them to get more bookings and better terms from theaters. These deals were either 50/50 splits or 70/30 after expenses (70 going to *Best*). They ended up making between $600 and $2,600 per screening, which is pretty good for a one-night event, especially considering that their per-screen average for their conventional theatrical was $2,385.50 for *a week-long run.*

They also discovered that the theaters knew what nights and times their membership would come out—either 7pm on Wednesday night or 8pm on a Thursday—it varied city-to-city and was very specific. (It is important to know your audience—and what their media consumption patterns are.)

Amy Sedaris in The Best and the Brightest

Until that point, they had accomplished everything without a trailer, which they finally got in mid-April. Within days it had 70,000 views on YouTube. This upped the activity on the website, got more volunteers involved, and helped boost awareness generally.

By the time of their official "theatrical" on June 24th they had already had 200 screenings in 24 cities/venues (with another four openings to coincide with the "theatrical"). Five of these previews transformed into week-long runs.

Ultimately, they made enough money from these screenings to pay for the expense of the operation—not a money-making operation—but they had a 28 venue theatrical release for no extra expense. As a result, they connected with their audience, created a way for the filmmakers to experience the film in the manner that they intended (with an audience) and raised awareness for the film. All of which together put a substantial dent in the overcrowded media landscape.

THEATRICAL PART 2—CONVENTIONAL THEATRICAL

New Video and Weiser engaged Marian Koltai-Levine of PMK to create a theatrical release for the film in New York and Los Angeles (Miami also came on board as part of Baldwin's sneak previews) for a fee of $50,000. New Video put up 50% of this fee), which included around $20,000 for print ads. The 50K also included the four-wall fees for the theaters in NY and Los Angeles. It made sense for *Best* to spend this money because they had stars in the film. Hence, they would get reviews as well as other forms of national press, such as Neil Patrick Harris on Conan O'Brien, Amy Sedaris on Letterman and John Hodgman on The Daily Show, among others.

Total gross for opening weekend—$4,771—hence the per-screen average for NY/LA: $2,385.50. Weiser told us, "There was no expectation of making our money back from the theatrical itself, but we hope it will all impact the bottom line DVD/VOD/digital sales."

A PDF of live event theatrical screenings can be found at http://www.sellingyourfilm.com/BAB-321.html.

Neil Patrick Harris in The Best and the Brightest

ADDITIONAL BENEFITS OF THE PREVIEW SCREENINGS.

Weiser: *One of the advantages of 200 sold-out screenings with appreciative and engaged audiences was that it made it easier for the team to accept the bad reviews that happened during the theatrical release.*

Koltai-Levine was also able to get Emerging Pictures on board to continue the theatrical into about 30 to 40 additional cities. I personally love the Emerging Pictures model, which has a resonance with what Baldwin was doing. Emerging Pictures has a relationship with about 100 theaters nationwide, in which they can deliver a digital "print/file" for no cost. In other words, they have eliminated all print costs (even BluRay) and created a network of theaters that are connected to audiences. In addition, if you have a live event after your screening, Emerging can net-cast this to any of their member theaters. All this costs is $1000 encoding fee and 70% of the box office; the filmmaker keeps the other 30%. This is an incredible opportunity for the right independent film. (Emerging is naturally choosy about what films they will take on as it has to make sense for their network of theaters.)

John Hodgman in The Best and the Brightest

WHAT IS THEATRICAL?

Because of this traditional theatrical, New Video and Koltai-Levine persuaded Baldwin and Weiser not to call the preview screenings "theatrical" because it would blow their premiere weekend and the press that they would get from that opening weekend.

Best illustrates more than any film the absurdity of what is considered "theatrical" by the film industry.

Best screened in 28 cities to 200 packed houses full of people who had gotten out of their homes to experience a film communally. Although these screenings were more successful than most independent "theatrical" releases in terms of reach and revenue, this was not considered a theatrical release. Weiser agreed with me that any time you screen your film in front of an audience, it is a theatrical screening. What does the specific venue or length of release matter? Weiser said, "We're in theaters. We're screening our film. We're theatrical."

THEATRICAL PART 3

The filmmakers are currently speaking with Todd Sklar and hope to be part of his Range Life tour in the fall of 2011. However, they don't want to charge admission for these screenings in an interesting twist. They only want potential audience members to show that they posted the trailer of *Best* to their Facebook page (or some such similar social media promotion) in order to spread awareness for the film. Weiser: "Ticket sales at screenings is not the monetization event; driving fans to DVD/VOD/Digital sales is the monetization event. It always has been."

DVD DIGITAL

DVD/VOD/DIGITAL are all being released day-and-date on August 16, 2011 with the only exception being hotel pay-per-view, which started in July. Netflix will follow at 28 days post-street date. New Video went with day-and-date in this manner to capitalize on the publicity created by the live event/theatrical release. I plan to report on these ancillary figures as they become available (it will probably take a year to get a real sense of what the result was).

FOREIGN DEAL

Foreign is being handled by Dan March at Echo Bridge. Weiser liked his candor. "Dan said 'I could try to promise you theatrical, but that isn't going to happen in this market.' In Dan's view, the best chance for sales for this film is to sell television internationally; theatrical sales, if any, would be gravy."

Weiser: *At the end of the day, one of three things is going to happen: (1) Best becomes a cult, viral hit and everybody gets their money back or more; (2) Best meets expectations and we get back some of our money; or (3) Best underperforms, my investors and I continue to have awkward moments at parties and try to make the best of it, but we all go back to our day jobs.*

Under 1, I will recognize that everything we did contributed to the result; I would consider doing everything "the next time" and, most importantly, I would budget for it.

Under 2, same answer, except that there probably isn't a next time for these particular investors. For myself as a producer, I need to come up with a different investment plan and a slightly different type of investor. I have to assume this is where we will end up, so I am working on that now.

Under 3, same answer, except that there probably isn't a next time for me and these particular investors at all.

LESSONS LEARNED

Lesson 1: A hybrid approach is best.

Weiser: *I have to say that what I've learned from this whole process is that, at least for now, the best bet for a film like ours is a hybrid approach to distribution, which combines some of the better elements of the "old system" (e.g., partnering with New Video and PMK), and some of the better aspects of the "new system" (the preview screenings). We have legit stars in Best, so we can employ some more traditional methods (enough P&A to get their stars on national televi-*

sion), but in a limited way (limit the $$) so as to make it a smart spend.

I think we all benefit from not just turning our films over to big distribution partners (like we did with Bigger, Stronger, Faster) unless they actually pay us for them. (Of course, we have a responsibility to ourselves and our investors to tighten our budgets and stick to them so this biz can make sense for everyone in the end). It's a crazy time for independent film, but opportunities are most prevalent during crazy times. I do still think Best has a real opportunity to break out. Only time will tell.

Lesson 2: Have a unique plan for your film.

Lesson 3: Have a back-up plan.

Weiser: *Don't forget to have a plan (and a back-up plan) and budget for marketing/distribution in case Fox Searchlight doesn't write you a big, fat check. I had a plan (to use tax credit dollars for the marketing/distribution plan) that didn't work out (investors wanted the money back). I think we've put together a pretty good back-up plan. We will see. The most successful people are those who are good at Plan B.*

Lesson 4: Know your audience before you make your film.

Weiser: *I've thought a lot about "finding your audience," and I think the better course is to know who your audience is before you make the film. In fact, don't make it unless you know your audience, where they are and how to get to them.*

L-R Peter Serafinowicz, Amy Sedaris, Bonnie Somerville,
Neil Patrick Harris in The Best and the Brightest

Adventures of Power

By Orly Ravid

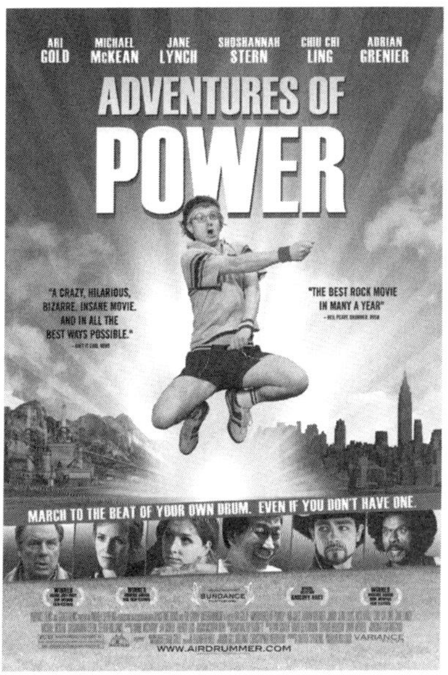

Adventures of Power, *directed by Ari Gold*

SYNOPSIS

Adventures of Power (Sundance 2008) is an award-winning comedy about an unemployed mine worker named Power who discovers an "underground railroad" of air-drummers, which leads him to change the world. It's *Rocky* for everyone who ever wanted to play music.

CAST

Starring Ari Gold (*Groove*), Adrian Grenier (*Entourage*), Jane Lynch (*Glee, The 40 Year Old Virgin*), Michael McKean (*This is Spinal Tap, A Mighty Wind*), Chiu Chi Ling (*Kung Fu Hustle*), Shoshannah Stern (*Weeds*), Jimmy Jean-Lous (*Heroes*), and Nick Kroll (*The Life & Times of Tim*).

SOUNDTRACK

Featuring an original soundtrack by Ethan Gold, alongside hits from Rush, Phil Collins, The Dazz Band and Mr. Mister.

PRESS QUOTES

"Spinal Tap caliber! Wonderful."
CHICAGO READER

"Totally awesome."
LOS ANGELES TIMES

"Platinum Level!"
CHICAGO SUN-TIMES

"An enthusiastic drums up!"
LOS ANGELES TIMES

"The best rock movie in many a year."
NEIL PEART, DRUMMER, RUSH

"One of the funniest films in recent years."
NEW YORK MAGAZINE

2008	Sundance Festival Premiere
2009	DIY Theatrical via Variance
2010	TFC comes on board, Ari brings on numerous consultants
2011	DVD, VOD, TV, Digital, and DIY Release

This chapter speaks to what went on with the film from its Sundance premiere in 2008 to its DVD release three years later and beyond to ongoing DIY distribution

WHY I CHOSE THIS FILM FOR OUR CASE STUDY BOOK

I selected *Adventures of Power* (AoP) because Ari Gold (writer/director/lead actor) has boundless energy when it comes to creating and promoting his work. He implemented a lot of smart and creative promotional techniques. At the same time, there's a lesson here about going to a festival with expectations that cannot always be met, and this case study shows the importance of having a distribution strategy that does not just rely on middlemen. When I asked Ari if I could include him and his film in this book he sent me an email: "Okay, I guess so—you can have my entire life's work." He sent me basically that; all of the work that he did to promote his film, all of his contact grids and everything in the interest of transparency and helping his fellow filmmakers. Some figures are not included because it is either too soon to note them or contractual commitments to other corporations prohibit their disclosure, but in those instances we give as approximate information as possible.

Below are some questions I asked of Ari, along with his answers. Some of the answers are from Anne Bernstein, Ari's VP of Production. So, here we go:

1. THE BEST FESTIVAL IN AMERICA AT WHICH TO PREMIERE

Adventures of Power premiered at the Sundance Film Festival in 2008. Sundance was and still is the best festival brand in America as far as consumer/audience awareness and distribution deals go. I remember seeing the film without knowing anyone involved (other than casually knowing producer Andrea Sperling). I really liked it. Super fun, funny, quirky, original. *Adventures of Power* is, in my opinion, the quintessential Sundance narrative—a fresh American voice ready to be discovered. The film was actually rushed to make it in time to screen at the festival; in fact, the version that showed at Sundance was not a final cut, and because Ari was so swamped with trying to finish the film he did not do any marketing or festival promotion. We (TFC) started working on the film in 2010, the year we launched. Veteran indie producer Gill Holland recommended us to Ari. We'd helped Gill with another one of his films, *Were the World Mine* (a gay musical that we also cover in the *Niche* chapter of this book.)

FESTIVALS & AWARDS

Official Selection	Sundance Film Festival
WINNER, Audience Award	Vail Film Festival
WINNER, Audience Award	Indie Memphis
WINNER, Grand Prize	San Antonio Film Festival
WINNER, Best Feature Film	TriMedia Film Festival
WINNER, Best Comedy	Philadelphia Film Festival
TOP-RATED U.S. COMEDY	Karlovy-Vary International Film Festival

** the film was also an official selection of dozens of other international festivals*

2. THE TRADITIONAL SALES AGENT / SALES COMPANY EXPERIENCE

Cassian Elwes of William Morris (Now WME) handled domestic sales. Shoreline was brought on by Cassian to handle international sales. On the domestic side of distribution, Screen Media was interested (a deal was not closed), and Think Film was interested but that company went out of business and filed for bankruptcy. Warner Independent had also expressed interest, but it shut down as well.

DISTRIBUTION SALES

Did you have a domestic sales rep? If so who?

> **Ari:** *Cassian Elwes at William Morris, but he became unavailable after we didn't make an instant sale at Sundance. Eventually we terminated and worked with TFC.*

Did you find William Morris effective?

> **Ari:** *They did not make a sale and it was difficult to get them on the phone to discuss interest, once the first few days of Sundance had passed.*

What percentage do you owe William Morris?

> **Ari:** *They took a piece of our foreign sales deal off the top, and continue to take a percentage of that. I honestly don't remember the percentage but I think the deal we signed with them was actually quite good* [note: standard agency commissions are 10% but it seems William Morris took 5%], *and then they basically forced us to give them an additional $7,500.00 out of our foreign sales.*

For how long will you continue to pay them?

> **Ari:** *The foreign sales deal is expiring and up for renewal now (2011). Domestic, we're clear.*

Shoreline handled foreign sales. Tell us more about them.

> **Ari:** *They have made a few sales and so far we haven't been paid. Recently however, Shoreline closed a deal with Lionsgate in the UK that includes DVD and Digital. The Shoreline deal capped expenses at $50,000 and they take a 22.5% fee.*

Do you know which markets Shoreline brought the film to in addition to the big ones most sales agents attend (AFM, Berlin's EFM, and the market at Cannes)?

> **Ari:** *Since their communication was limited, I can't say for sure. I did visit their suite in Berlin and found the film for sale there, though I don't know who they were talking to. I never did. I met a lot of foreign distributors in my travels and was never able to confirm that the references I passed to them were actually used.*

Were there any overall sales outside the US—(e.g. all rights including theatrical, DVD, TV)?

> **Ari:** *Japan, Australia, UK, Germany.*

Were there Foreign TV sales only? If so, how much?

> **Ari:** *Turkey and Israel.*

What were the deals like and what have the results been?

> **Ari:** *Honestly it's been like pulling teeth to find out what's going on. I found out we were on DVD in Germany—dubbed into German, no less!—because I have friends in Berlin who saw it in stores. But we haven't made a dime from that, and*

I wanted to get more information about the sales efforts and value, but the latest reporting is not in yet, and Ari was not given that much information, so it could not make it into this book. What I can say is that in aggregate the foreign sales (before July 2011) totaled approximately $90,000. After expenses being recouped, the sales agent's fee taken off the top and the extra kickback to William Morris, Ari netted between $2,000-$3,000. Everyone made more money than Ari or the investors via the foreign sales.

3. DIY THEATRICAL: LESSONS LEARNED—THE PROS & CONS

Ari hired Dylan Marchetti's company Variance Films to do the theatrical release and he worked with Range Life on the event/semi-theatrical.

CONVENTIONAL THEATRICAL

LIVE EVENT THEATRICAL

Did you do traditional theatrical, and if so, how much time did you spend to set it up?

> **Ari:** *I spent about four months setting it up.*

How much did you spend on the theatrical?

> **Ari:** *$150,000.* [Ari thinks that $20,000 went to prints.]

Did you use a service company?

> **Ari:** *Variance Films.*

How long was the theatrical run?

Ari: *About six weeks.*

How many cities were full-week runs?

Ari: *Eight.*

How many cities were one-night events in traditional theatrical venues?

Ari: *None.*

The box office grosses were disappointing but the campaign did at least kickstart awareness for the film's remaining distribution.

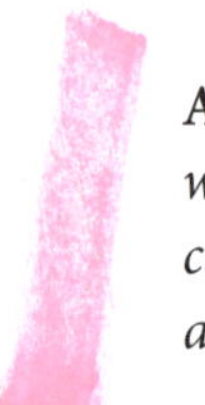

Ari: *We did best in Portland, Oregon. It was the only place we were able to outreach into the community properly because I was there for a few days, speaking on the radio and at schools.*

ALTERNATIVE THEATRICAL (INCLUDES NON-, SEMI- AND COMMUNITY THEATRICAL)

In how many cities did you have alternative theatrical screenings?

Ari: *15.* [Ari did this via Range Life.]

If there is a separate number from conventional theatrical—how much did you spend to book your alternative theatrical release?

Ari: *$1,500.*

How much did you gross on your alternative theatrical release?

Ari: *$800.*

To book college campus screenings, TFC referred Present Pictures, aka Festival Indies, to Ari after hearing good things about them from Peter Broderick and another producer. The cost was $3,000 (plus 20% of bookings revenue) to cover their expenses and presentation at NACA (National Association for College Activities), but they were not able to secure bookings so it was ultimately a failed effort. They said it was hard to book the film because it was not big enough, although they felt the outreach should at least help ancillaries. Present Pictures seems to have adjusted their business in light of realizing the smaller films were not working as well as the one that started their business release, their own 2008 Sundance film called *Good Dick*. Sadly, Ari also lost money on that effort. Ari's take on the experience: "They behaved exactly like a foreign sales agent. Their risk and expenses were covered, before the filmmakers. As usual, the filmmakers took all the risk."

Range Life worked on the hybrid theatrical release in tandem with the traditional theatrical. What was your experience with them?

Anne Bernstein: *Range Life got us screenings, but it is hard to tell what came of it. We tried to connect with the schools directly, before and after the screenings—to promote and also to get feedback, but it was beyond difficult. Range Life booked the screenings, but when I contacted them about promoting them, my efforts were in vain. We organized a lot of charity screenings on our own and this was much more satisfying—we had direct contact with the organizers and Ari often did a Skype Q&A with the audience afterwards, always mentioning the text-to-join number and getting a lot of new subscribers for our mailing list. We tried to make this* *happen with the Range Life screenings but, again, couldn't make it work.*

Ari shared with us his experience in handling publicity and he also speaks further to this later on in his interview with us:

Ari: *Having never done [a theatrical tour] before, I thought "OK let's do it, let's do what an indie [theatrical distributor] would do." But what I didn't realize was how much work goes into putting a movie in theaters than just getting it into a theater. Consistently in our theatrical release, we would do better on the last day than we would on the first day which was a sign that in a sense we were doing the right thing because word was spreading in each town, but because the way the theaters are, they determine whether a film will continue its run within the first 48 hours so that didn't work in our favor. I would come into a town on Friday when the film would open to try and get some press but [articles] didn't run until Sunday or Monday and by then they [the theater] had already cancelled the extension of the run. It wasn't until my last city, Portland, Oregon, that I realized we had structured this incorrectly in the sense that I had to be in each city at least a week or more ahead of time to do press.*

At the same time, the local newspapers have all been hard hit by staff cuts and we couldn't get the film reviewed locally. We were playing their theater, but we weren't deemed press worthy because we weren't a mainstream release and that is frustrating. Studio indies have the muscle of the studio marketing and publicity machine behind them, they can force a review to be done and we didn't and that is when I realized I had to turn my focus away from mainstream press and doing what a studio machine would do, instead I concentrated on connecting directly with the people of those communities. That's what's good about the Internet, you can really

ADVENTURES OF SHAMELESS PROMOTING: FUN WITH SOCIAL NETWORK & VIRAL MARKETING—WORK ARI CHOSE TO DO ON HIS OWN

Since the film did not sell at Sundance, along with most of the films caught up in the 2008 distribution upheaval, Ari set about DIY distribution. As mentioned above, he worked with Variance and Range Life on the theatrical/semi-theatrical, but it was not a financial success. The theatrical, however, did give the film the profile that we at TFC utilized later to secure home video, digital and broadcast distribution, as well as feeding the DIY distribution that Ari is now employing as well. But Ari was clear that even while he was working with Variance on the theatrical, he had already begun to do his own social networking and viral marketing.

Mailing list sign-ups	12,778
Twitter followers	3,101
Facebook fans	105,343

Social Networking stats as of June 2011

FACEBOOK & TWITTER

Regarding the Facebook fans and Twitter followers etc., how much of that was going on at Sundance before or soon after the festival vs. in tandem with the theatrical? How about since then? In other words, how do you and Ari view the building of the audience and fandom for this film?

> **Anne:** *Facebook fans were a combination of ad campaign and organic growth—the large majority came from a great ad campaign. Twitter came after Sundance. Adventures of Power only had a placeholder page on the web at Sun-*

dance—the website didn't happen for a while.

When we interviewed Ari, he talked about his observation that Facebook limits the reach of one's news feed that goes to one's Facebook fan base if one is not paying for ads. I asked Anne to elaborate on this and on their overall experience with Facebook.

Anne: *If the only way to harness the power of Facebook is to pay and pay and pay, it stops making sense at some point, no? Things used to spread more organically; the new system favors cash too heavily.*

I know that Facebook was recently at Cannes and took part in a panel on Independent Film Distribution. This is an exciting time for independent film and DIY distribution. Integration with our Social Media Networks is an obvious and integral part of this distribution process. Facebook will play a huge role in how effectively we, and other independent filmmakers, can distribute our films. Distrify has a widget that allows us to sell our film directly from our Facebook page. We shared this information with Facebook and hoped that they would want to support independent film and pave the way for effective DIY film distribution on Facebook. Our basic request was to allow us to effectively reach our fans.

We can't reach all (or even a decent percentage) of our fans. I don't think this issue is limited to our campaign; the news feed seems to be leaving a lot of users unhappy and missing out on things that they wanted to know. Take this event, for example. If fans of Adventures of Power *had happily been reading the updates, but hadn't clicked or interacted in a few weeks when the change was made to the news feed, they are now no longer getting updates.*

The ad specialist we spoke with at Facebook suggested that we try doing Sponsored Stories, as in PAID, in order to reach more of our fans. Well, first we had to swallow the fact that we can only reach around 20% of our fans if we don't do a Sponsored Story, but what makes even less sense is that if Ari pays for a Sponsored Story, he still can't reach even half of his fans. Moreover, spending on a Sponsored Story after we have spent a good deal of time and money advertising and collecting fans simply seems wrong.

I feel as though I should mention what happened with another page of mine, to further illustrate this flawed new news feed. I created a page for one of my favorite foods from Germany called Käsespätzle. This page grew over a fairly short period of time to over 24,000 fans. I would post a photograph maybe once every two months, but did nothing else. I never advertised. People visited the page a lot, and a healthy and funny debate arose over how to pronounce, spell, prepare, and eat Käsespätzle, and where they are originally from (south of Germany or Western Austria.) When the news feed changed on Facebook, this page stopped growing overnight. I had seen constant, organic growth over the course of a year and a half, and then nothing, from one day to the next. When I asked the specialist why this was happening, he suggested that the fans had lost interest. All of a sudden. From one day to the next.

At the time when Ari placed his ads on Facebook, the news feed was still working—meaning a healthy percentage of his fans were still getting updates. Then the news feed changed. Facebook has our advertising money, and we can no longer reach our fans. Basically, if a Facebook user didn't click on an item in the news feed in the few weeks leading up to when the change was made—if that user didn't interact with someone in that time frame—that person or page will no longer be in their news feed. I don't know about you, but I am a pretty passive Facebook user. I don't typically click on people's news feed items. I just read them in the feed. We tried to get them to work with us on this issue, but so far (surprise!) we haven't had any luck.

Here's what's going on with Facebook's news feed. According to Inside Facebook, Facebook "changed the options in its news feed settings so users either 'Show posts from: friends and Pages you interact with the most' or from 'all of your friends and Pages.' Some users have unknowingly been defaulted to the first option, causing lot of content to be hidden from them without their knowledge." One way of looking at this is that Facebook perhaps made this default to the first option to eleviate the glut of messages coming in for real "power users." What Anne is discussing above is a kind of collateral damage to people with Fan Pages, who don't have a daily or weekly interaction with all of their fans. Given the fact that Facebook told Anne and Ari that they could get back to their fans by buying ads, however, another way of looking at this is that Facebook was just looking for ways to make money.

Facebook newsfeed drama aside, when it comes to social network marketing, it is best to build community and a campaign around a film before its premiere, especially if the film is at such a big press and buzz-generating festival. If nothing else, it helps the film's distribution potential and the director's career. I think this case study shows Ari's amazing ability to create community around a film and a potential to sell to an audience. Any delay in doing that only mitigates that potential. Ari agrees with this as well and speaks to this in his interview.

One also has to remember that the number of Facebook fans or Twitter followers you have doesn't necessarily correlate to the potential number of customers. 37% of Twitter followers are more likely to purchase a brand after becoming a follower, compared to 27% of email subscribers and only 17% of Facebook fans, according to September 2010 analysis from ExactTarget. Research conducted by Applied Predictive Technologies, a software company that analyzes the impact of social media programs, suggests that brands see an average revenue boost of 2% from programs on social platforms such as Facebook Places and Foursquare.

VIRAL VIDEOS, IPHONE APPS & EBLASTS

> **Anne:** *We updated the website when I came on board (in 2010) so that we weren't so dependent on our programmer to make changes—so that we are nimble and can change it up as needed. We can add new videos and promote our initiatives, (for example the Air-Drum Battle). It has been a tireless, multi-pronged effort to gain fans; YouTube, Facebook, Twitter, initiatives such as the Auction and Air-Drum Battle, asking friends to Tweet and the radio and college radio tours.*

One of the first tenets of Ari Gold's "Good Promotional Techniques" is to build an email list, and he began to do this during the semi-theatrical and theatrical screenings. Seems pretty straightforward, right? But check this out: Ari attached a short video to the front of the feature at the semi-theatrical and theatrical screenings that included the text-to-join number, whereby one texts their email address to a Google Voice number that he set up…it was (213) 290-DRUM [213.290.3786]…and, at the time of this book's publication, it still works, even though he has to manually copy and paste the emails into his master list. The video alone was extremely effective, but when Ari was also present at the screenings, or when he did a live Skype Q&A, he was able to get almost all in the audience to sign up. Truly unique and impressive.

Ari is a great promoter; he's diligent and creative. Here are some other examples (we're skipping to Ari's promotion of the DVD here):

Okay, I guess so - you can have my my entire life's work. And an air-drumming App too!

I asked my distributor to cut the price of my DVD in half for pre-order. Do it. "One of the funniest films in recent years" —New York Magazine. Includes all my short films, interviews, and more. Laugh and cry and laugh again. http://amzn.to/eyJBG0

And, since life isn't complete without starring in an **iPhone App**, we made an air-drumming App too. It costs nothing, except your arms will get beefy. Seriously. http://tinyurl.com/4ccpc9m

The Videos: I'm making 2 a week for Youtube; today's is extra-special, an anthem by my brother Ethan Gold from the soundtrack for Adventures of Power. Tell us what you think. http://tinyurl.com/4ccpc9m

LAST BUT NOT LEAST, if you'd like to help with my Vh1 auction to support music education for disadvantaged kids, write me back! **Ringo Starr, Metallica, Rush, Judas Priest, Ke$ha, The Ramones, Pink Martini, Ween,** and many more have joined me. What about you?

And in case you were wondering, you're getting this email because you are a **SHALWUM (a.k.a. Shining Hope for Ari's Life's Work to Uplift the Masses),** masses who clearly (if you read the news) desperately need to see these films, but won't without your help.

Please procrastinate on your homework BY TELLING ALL YOUR FRIENDS ABOUT "ADVENTURES OF POWER", "The best rock movie in many a year" (according to Neil Peart)!

OFFICIAL SITE—http://AdventuresOfPower.com

OWN THE MAGIC—http://amzn.to/eyJBG0

"Spinal Tap caliber"—Chicago Reader. "An enthusiastic Drums Up!"—LA Times. "Crazy hilarious"—Ain't It Cool News.

MY YOUTUBE CHANNEL (2 new videos every week!)—http://youtube.com/arigoldfilms

FACEBOOK—http://facebook.com/adventuresofpower

TWITTER—http://twitter.com/arigold

AOP/Vh1 SAVE THE MUSIC AUCTION—http://AdventuresOfPower.com/auction

Click on my dad. Seriously.

Ari explains why and what he did to support the film on his own:

> **Ari:** *The traditional publicity that came with our DVD release was not able to get us much press and not on rock music stations. So Anne and I bought an email list of every*

radio station in the US and Canada and we emailed them all. I had to use a spam email program to do that and probably about 15% of the emails made it through past a filter and then to actually be read. But it lead to maybe 40-50 radio interviews with college and traditional radio that we got completely on our own. I got an email from one of the colleges after I did the interview with them and they said our movie was the number one movie rental on campus. No one would have heard of the movie much less rent or buy it if I hadn't done that interview.

Ari shared a lot of what he did:

Ari: *For your study and collaboration here is my master plan for the movie above-and-beyond standard distributor "dumping" of a DVD into the food chain. You might want to bookmark these in an Adventures of Power folder in your browser, if you're curious to follow along.*

I was.

Ari: *These are separate from the jobs that have either been done by or are being done by* Phase4, *(the US Distributor after the theatrical/semi-theatrical was long finished),* LBi *(ePR, covered below), and* 42West *(Phase4's PR firm and one that I have known to do a great job for bigger releases). This is me, Anne, and* Susan Boyer [a social network marketing consultant TFC referred based on Roadside Attractions' recommendation], *making something happen.*

As mentioned above, Ari and Anne created an 835-line grid called "Radio Spam,"which included contacts at radio stations across the country. It's too big of a grid to show in this book, but in terms of the information source, Anne Bernstein shared with me that she signed up for Musicians Atlas, *and she recommends it as a resource if one is looking to target radio stations and bloggers. It's where she and Ari got their huge spam list.* [Anne notes that there may be other similar resources.]

They contacted commercial and college radio stations and national and regional press across the entire country. They were often ignored, but they also often got press which did yield results and which Ari speaks to in his interview

> **Ari:** *We sent out about 800 emails to radio stations (many genres) in the US, and 750 emails to college radio stations across the US and Canada. From this we secured around 40 radio interviews. We did promos and giveaways [DVDs and AOP sweatbands]. With regard to radio interviews, it is virtually impossible to track how many DVD sales or Netflix rentals, etc., result from each occurrence. But it takes virtually no effort to send out a bulk email. The lion's share of the work is following up with the DJs and programmers who respond, setting up interviews, sending promo materials and doing the interview.*

Ari did note that mainstream press seems generally uninterested in smaller indie releases, and this certainly seems evident to us.

Ari and Anne also researched, reached out to and had very organized grids for press contacts, their auction work with VH1's Save the Music, and their viral videos work so that they could efficiently and thoroughly do a lot of and track all their outreach.

Ari's concluding thoughts on DIY Marketing:

> **Ari:** *On the one hand, I can do all of the work that a studio marketing department can do, at home on my laptop and with a camera. But the flipside is, I have to, and where will I find the time to do, my next work, my next film, when I have to spend so much time reaching the fans of the film I just made? It would be great to be one of the few doing this inside of the system or who was plucked out of Sundance to be the next "made man" and you go to premiere and the press just*

Here are two more samples of Ari's Promos that he sent to his lists:

From: "Ari Gold" <ari@arigoldfilms.com>
Date: May 19, 2011 9:25:26 AM PDT
Subject: german attack video

Here's my new video from Berlin, which is essential to understand world history. Pass it on.

Also, you've got five more days to enter the http://AirDrumBattle.com and I'll send you drums, "Adventures of Power" costumes, and my love. Do it for world peace.

As always, please buy copies (for all your friends) of the movie and all my short films here: http://amzn.to/eyJBG0

Here's my video thank-you from Germany:

You also created mobile phone Apps. What happened with those in terms of distribution?

> **Ari:** *It was done by Stonehenge. We got lots of downloads but no film sales.*

TFC got Stonehenge to create the initial basic version of the *Adventure of Power* iPhone App itself for free, but then Ari paid extra for an Android version ($1,500 on contract). They later updated the Apps to include a drum component ($650 for the iPhone version, $400 for the Android version). So the total price for Ari was $2,550. And Stonehenge was to get 15% of the gross of the in-App film sales. After Apple's 30% cut, they were set to get 55% of the sales revenue. They ended up getting 765 downloads for the iPhone version and 1,392 for the Android version. Interestingly, second to the US, the country with the most demand for the App so far is South Korea. Other countries with the film's App users are: United Kingdom, Malaysia, Thailand, Sweden, Ireland, Netherlands, Italy and Germany (in that order). But no one has purchased the film from inside the App.

TFC's Creative Director David Averbach weighed in on iPhone Apps for films:

> **David:** *I love the idea of an interactive App for a feature film. No doubt that it enhances the brand…these Apps came out at a time when even just being able to say that your film had a iPhone App was worth a lot in terms of bragging rights. I suspect part of the reason why Stonehenge was willing to do the initial App for free was to, ahem, drum up new business. Earlier this year they were offering a deal to filmmakers looking to create a similar App for well under $1K. A major problem, however, was that their approach to content delivery in some of their Apps, at least from a technical standpoint, was a bit flawed. When the* Adventures of Power *App for the iPhone was updated to version 1.1, they embedded the entire film inside the App—which appeared in the iTunes App Store as a free download—and then gave the user the opportunity to unlock the film through a $9.99 in-App purchase. So what's wrong with this approach? The file was over 1GB in size! So the user had to download a*

huge App even if they did not want to watch the film. My iPhone has only 8GB of total storage, and it has a lot on there already, so I never was able to get my computer to sync the upgrade to the App to my phone due to space limitations. I suppose you can count me as one of those 765 users, but I never actually got to use version 1.1. Of course not everybody had this particular problem, but still, a mandatory huge download just to get the App would not be the way I would have gone.

Then there's the matter of no one having actually purchased the film through the App. Stonehenge felt that the availability of the DVD and other digital formats hindered sales. Sure, one might dismiss the whole concept of a feature in a mobile App, wondering, "Why would anyone pay $10 to watch a full-length movie that you can only watch on your phone?" But there is more to the story. I think the concept of the App was actually ahead of its time, and if you look at the explosion of tablet devices in the past year, it's something to really keep an eye on. In theory, it's great that mobile rights can be negotiated separately for a film, but since nowadays you can get Netflix streaming and iTunes rentals on your phone as well, the distinction gets a little murky, and the end-user doesn't know or care about that distinction anyway. Frankly, a company like Stonehenge, in all fairness, probably had almost no choice but to embed their film in the code because the cost of remotely storing and delivering content to a mobile device, whether it be streaming or downloading, is still prohibitive, although it's getting cheaper and chapter these days. The only thing still exciting about Apps is that they are worldwide basically by default, so if Stonehenge or somebody else can overcome the technical and cost-related issues, it could be the fastest way to get your film out to all parts of the globe. [Note: TFC is releasing an App for its FestSelects™Best LGBT Shorts collections.]

4. WHAT SOCIAL NETWORKING & VIRAL MARKETING WORK ARI CHOSE TO DO WITH SERVICES AND CONSULTANTS

Ari Gold worked with Susan Boyer, Believe Limited and LBi on Internet, online and grassroots outreach.

Phase4 uses 42West for overall publicity and so they were involved too. LBi ended up being hired by Phase4, whereas Ari paid Believe and Susan Boyer directly.

SUSAN BOYER

> **Ari:** *Susan Boyer (the social network marketing consultant TFC referred) gave good advice and support. We were on our own building our online community. She had good advice for us regarding how to clarify our marketing message.*
>
> **Anne***: Susan really helped to boil things down to what was important. Ari and I both tend to want to bite off more than we can chew; she helped to streamline the operation and keep us focused. She joined us on conference calls with Phase4, LBi, and 42West. She organized our online ad campaign with Jivox (although I'm not sure how effective that was), and introduced us to landing pages for our website and other marketing tools. We were all juggling a lot of things at that point—the DVD release party, the VH1 auction (finding donors, coordinating), the press push, the online presence on our website and ads, our social networks— and Susan worked hard to stay on top of things. With a little bit of perspective now, I see how much craziness was going on and Susan managed to keep up with us. We are a small, hands-on operation with a passionate captain at the helm (Ari), who has limitless time and energy to devote to his projects. We had ambitious goals and we met them all—having a DVD release become a news item is a Herculean task, and we pulled it off. We got Onitsuka Tiger to*

sponsor the event, got the Honey Brothers to perform (this was not easy, in fact), teamed up with VH1 Save the Music (which Susan secured), and launched our online auction at the event (which went on to raise enough money to save a school's music program). We spearheaded our own press campaign, redesigned and optimized our website with landing pages, and learned a ton about how to do it better the next time!

Susan explained about her work overall and her work on the Jivox campaign that she initiated:

Susan: *I began working with filmmaker Ari Gold on the DVD release of his comedy rock parody,* Adventures of Power, *distributed by Phase 4 Films in January 2011. In general, I believe I helped bring some strategic discipline to the process.*

There were some funds in the marketing cap reserved for street teams—kids who would fan out on college campuses with t-shirts and buttons—but the comparison case studies were for Juno and Napoleon Dynamite, both of which had $100 million-plus theatrical runs. We got those funds reallocated toward a rich media ad campaign.

We used an ad-serving agency called Jivox in San Francisco to run the targeted, contextual campaign. The targeting came in site selection; we chose web sites that skewed males, ages 14-54. Once Jivox gave us a list of about 200 sites that met those criteria, I pruned all of the sports-oriented sites and added a few more entertainment sites to the mix.

The context came in the key words and phrases that would trigger the ad serving, which included the name of our movie and movies we thought were compatible ('Adventures of Power,' 'Spinal Tap,' ' Napoleon Dynamite') all of our talent ('Ari Gold,' 'Adrian Grenier,' 'Jane Lynch,' etc.), music-orient-

ed words and phrases ('air-drumming,' 'drumming,' 'Rush,' 'Neil Peart') and so on.

The trick was to select words and phrases that would deliver folks who might actually convert to sales and that wouldn't cannibalize all of our impressions or clicks (every time an ad is served up on a page, it counts as an impression). For instance, we didn't include the term 'Glee' in our key words, even though Jane Lynch is in the movie because we thought that search term would cannibalize our impressions and that 'Glee' fans would not necessarily convert to sales for Adventures of Power.

Once we had our site selection and key words, we chose what are known as the ad units, meaning the actual rich media players. One player, for example, would expand on the page when scrolled over, however, it could only be served up on sites that accepted that type of player. Another player had social media buttons, driving to our Facebook and Twitter pages (Ari is a brilliant social networker), while yet another player was very sales-oriented, with buttons that drove to our Amazon page.

Ari produced specific creative for each ad unit; the Adrian Grenier ad unit, which would be served up on search terms 'Adrian Grenier,' 'Entourage,' and 'The Honey Brothers' (Ari and Adrian's band), started with a clip of Adrian from the movie, then segued into a snippet of the trailer, concluding with the 'Now available on Amazon' sales message.

We produced four distinct ad units: one each for Adrian Grenier, Jane Lynch, drumming/air-drumming, and one for the deaf community, featuring hearing-impaired co-star Shoshannah Stern. The Shoshannah ad unit was completely close-captioned for the hearing-impaired.

Once we had our sites selected, key words defined and ad units created, we had to think about what would hap-

pen when folks clicked on the ad; where would they land? I recommended that we create distinct landing pages corresponding to each ad unit, which in turn linked directly to Amazon. Anne Bernstein executed all of these landing pages featuring targeted clips and bullets (for instance, the Jane Lynch landing page included one of her scenes from the movie, as well as sales messaging geared toward her fans).

The campaign ran for about three weeks, during which time close to one million impressions were served up and we achieved a click rate of between 1.5%-3%, higher than average for this type of campaign. In general, these types of campaigns are for brand-building and not direct sales, but through the creation of targeted ad units and landing pages, we did our best to convert clicks to sales.

BELIEVE LIMITED

One of the reasons Ari has been able to widen his fan base is that he is constantly making new content available to his fans. His targeted marketing approach includes actively producing one video a week and putting them up on his YouTube channel. Ari and Anne hired Believe Limited to help them promote these videos, which include vlogs, music videos, clips, outtakes and deleted scenes, on the web.

How much did you spend on consultants?

Ari/Anne: *We hired Believe (Matt and Ryan Gielen) to run our YouTube campaign. Part of what they do is to advise us as to what is good YouTube content, when to release it, etc. We spent between $0 and $1000 on each video we release. Believe's fee is a portion of this spend and the rest essentially goes to getting views for the videos.*

Explain the YouTube stats and your work with Believe. What activity led to more views?

> **Ari:** *We have grown our YouTube page to over 2,000 subscribers with Believe's help. This number is good, not amazing, but it continues to grow—slowly and steadily, which ultimately could be the best way to go. If each of these subscribers is a real hard-core follower, then they are very valuable. We spend on videos and do targeted campaigns, but I don't really understand how this works—Believe handles this. Then, if the video gets picked up by a blog gawker.tv or a Rush blog, they get anywhere from 500-150,000 views. We release a new video every week. Some videos are AoP-related or clips/outtakes from the movie. Other videos are not related to AoP at all.*

We also asked Believe about this:

> **Believe Limited:** *We set out to brand Ari Gold the filmmaker, as well as his film* Adventures of Power *as new and exciting voices in the digital landscape.*
>
> *YouTube averages 35+ hours of video uploaded every minute, and receives over 2 Billion video views daily. Through our huge network and outreach, we got* Adventures of Power *onto the front page of YouTube three times, next to names like Jay Z and Transformers.*
>
> *We helped Ari's videos jump in front of a billion other videos, to introduce his film to YouTube's enormous audience, and the full list of results are below. We believe being an independent should not mean marketing like one. Let us introduce you to the entire world.*

Playlists on Ari's YouTube channel

Can you explain how you do this? How many films do you work on each year?

> **Believe:** *We use our massive networks on YouTube and Facebook, as well as our relationships with outside websites to drive demographic and location-targeted people to each video. We typically work on two to three outside films and several of our own projects each year. We believe in devoting our attention to projects we really believe in and we give each project the attention it deserves.*

Is YouTube your key focus platform?

> **Believe:** *For 99 Problems we took a multi-tiered approach. Our first step was a small and targeted ad buy. This landed the video onto the front pages of YouTube where it was exposed to millions of viewers. Our next step was to share the video with our YouTube network of 1M subscribers and friends. We also did targeted outreach to new media sites, blogs and on Facebook. In conjunction with this promotion netting the views, intelligent titling, tagging, and describing the video, we were able to get the video to be the #2 search result for "99 problems," which continues to net thousands of views per month.*

YouTube and Facebook are our main focus when working with films. We have our largest networks there, but if a project is not exactly right for YouTube, we have relationships with many different types of websites and formulate plans that work for each individual project.

With respect to the Drum Channel contest, how well did this go? What were the results?

Believe: *The campaign went well from our perspective because Drum Channel advertised at no cost to their entire audience—tens of thousands of young drummers (a large part of Ari's core audience). Since Ari and Anne managed the contest I don't have more particulars.*

Believe's noted victories regarding *Adventures of Power*:

- got Ari's videos to appear on the front page (homepage) of YouTube three times
- got official *Adventures of Power* trailer onto YouTube's front page—exposure to millions, and has accumulated over 100K views to date.
- 1.5 Million + views across all videos (500% more than previous 3 years combined)
- Over 50,000 community engagements (favorites, likes, comments)
- Over 2,500 new subscribers or a 1,500% increase across two channels
- Created Marketing Plan for each video as well as for the campaign as a whole
- Incorporated branding to drive DVD sales, including in-house graphic design
- Helped create and implement viral campaigns outside of YouTube, such as the extremely popular Air Drum competition with major co-sponsor, DrumChannel.com
- Made AriGoldFilms a YouTube partner, allowing branding and monetization. Income on all videos!

One example is a video Ari did entitled "99 Problems—99 Cents" in which highlights 99 problems for 99 kids who take over the 99 Cents Only store for Halloween.

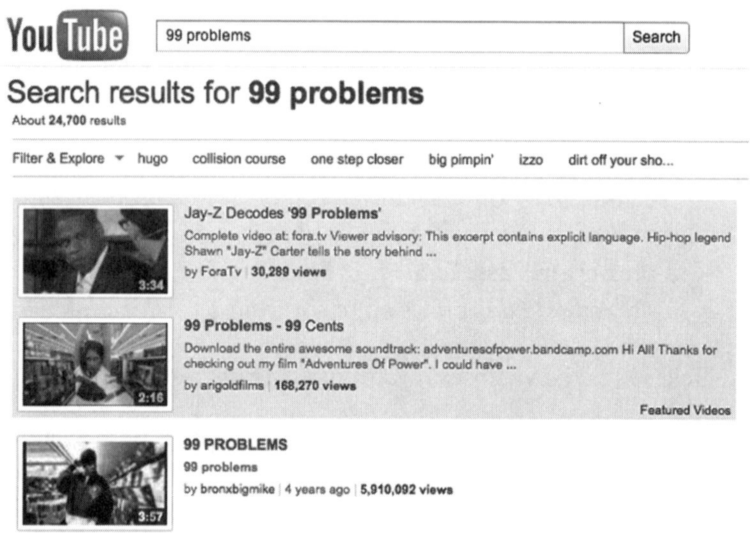

99 Problems - 99 Cents *video appears in "Featured Videos"*
as #2 when a search for "99 problems" is conducted.
"Featured Videos" which involves no ad buy, is a ranking
that is determined by a number of factors, including
but not limited to number of views.

Believe: *The YouTube partner program is an exclusive program that allows pages to add multiple banners, make revenue from their videos and allows their videos to be featured throughout YouTube. We do not have the revenue info from AdSense.* [Note: it violates Google's privacy policy to publish that info—doing so could cost Ari the partnership, which removes all custom branding and ads!] *In order to earn AdSense revenue from videos on YouTube, you must be a partner. Unfortunately, YouTube does not give hard numbers on what it takes to become a partner, they only say that "You regularly upload videos that are viewed by*

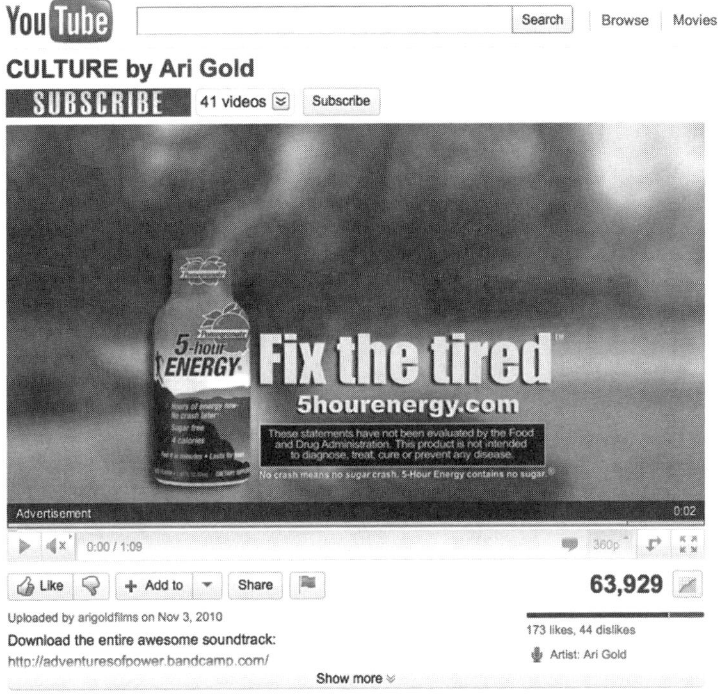

This ad is part of the YouTube AdSense program

Believe noted that the real money is only made with millions of views, otherwise it's just small money. I know the exact sum, but I cannot disclose it in this book (all I will say is that it is three-figures.) The bigger initiative was to get people to buy the DVD, where the filmmakers typically make the most money. While this initiative was not solely responsible for increased sales it was a key component. Anne notes that since this promotion started the film sold out on Amazon on the first day. The Netflix DVD units jumped as well (1,600). Ari set up an Affiliate program with Amazon and tracked how sales were generated. Believe noted they developed an audience for Ari Gold, not just his film, so he can remarket to this audience for each of his next films. Long term branding.

> **Believe:** *Another goal was to brand the film and Ari, and to begin building an online audience. Ari wanted a Big Lebowski, long-tail promotion that would get people buying/renting/streaming the film for years, making it a cult classic, as opposed to a goal of generating huge DVD sales. The plummeting DVD market and the grassroots budget factored heavily into the equation. What we're seeing and what we will continue to see is Ari and Adventures of Power becoming a lasting film, as opposed to most indies that hit Sundance and attempt to launch, only to end up on a shelf or fading into the ether. This is in large part because of the social media efforts, including the YouTube campaign. The challenge, of course, is how to quantify that, especially when we're only six months out from release date...*
>
> *In the new world of social media marketing and self distribution it's not enough to just make the film a success. It's essential to brand the filmmaker and develop an audience for the filmmaker to carry from project to project. There is no better spokesman for a film than the person who has poured his heart, soul, time and money into a project. A filmmaker's job is no longer done when they deliver final cut.*

Believe also worked with the other companies involved in the DVD distribution to maximize strategy around the release of the

DVD.

Please explain how many videos you have worked with? What were the differences between them? What worked and what did not work? How do you think your work compares with the rest of the work done to promote the film?

Believe: *We have released over 45 videos to date and are continuing to consult and work with Ari and Anne on a daily basis with regard to their YouTube channel and video release schedule. We've found that what works best are personal vlogs and unique videos (such as music videos), released in conjunction with the more branded (AoP) content. By supporting the main content and message we want to push (Adventures of Power/buy DVD) with additional content such as vlogs and music videos, we keep the audience coming back each week to see what Ari will release next. This also helps create interest, not just in the film, but also in Ari the filmmaker. Varying the content even slightly made a big difference week to week. We wouldn't want to compete with the rest of the AoP team; we just know we demystify and manage the entire YouTube experience and introduce films and filmmakers to huge audiences they would never reach without our facilitation.*

OUTREACH AND INTERNET MARKETING

TFC had recommended LBi to handle ePR, and they were ultimately hired by Phase4. LBi's strength is in leveraging highly trafficked sites and seeding those sites with exclusive clips and trailers in a way that may not always organically grow the fan base for a film, but which helps make a good impression in the market place and get the film's marketing out there. I have worked with them over the years and found them very useful, mostly on the B2B side.

LBi: *To promote the* Adventures of Power *DVD release, LBi executed a comprehensive ePR campaign. As part of* *the campaign we placed clips, coordinated reviews and ran giveaways across a variety of entertainment-focused sites. As a result, we garnered coverage on 58 websites and blogs, including Yahoo! Movies, Moviefone, USA Today, Univision and MovieWeb. We didn't include impressions for this campaign. Our total uniques number is the sum of all of the site traffic on all of the sites we got coverage on. Our formula for each sites' impressions is:*

[site traffic ÷ 30] × [number of days live on the site]

You can download the report from LBi by going to http://www.sellingyourfilm.com/AOP-46.html.

Anne: *When we first started working with LBi, Ari wasn't posting very much at all, but every time LBi posted, we lost fans. Their tone was so cheesy… We had a talk with them and they admitted this was the case—first they tried to re-tool their posts and then they redirected a portion of the budget to a paid ad campaign on Facebook. I am grateful that they (LBi) were nimble enough to change mid-campaign and listen to our feedback. They were probably not the right team for our Facebook campaign, but I feel I must note that they were professional and a pleasure to work with.*

Distribution, it's almost like dating isn't it?

PUBLICITY MARKETING COSTS AND ANALYTICS

Costs associated with Susan Boyer's Marketing Consultation Services

- Our original deal with Susan was for $7,500 paid in real money. A high-end drum kit valued at $2,000 was final payment for the initial contract. Susan gave the drum kit to her son.
- Susan requested/required an additional payment of $1,800 to run/plan the DVD release party/event.

- We also hired Susan to do additional press outreach after the release and paid her another $3,000.
- The total amount for Susan Boyer was $12,300 + drum kit ($2,000 value).
- The Jivox video enabled web buy cost $15,000 and was paid for (and recouped) by Phase4.

Anne: *With Susan, we tried to coordinate with Phase4 and their efforts with LBi and 42West.*

Phase4 spent approximately $35,000 on LBi, Jivox, and some other outreach efforts. The overall marketing budget for the DVD/Digital release (paid for and recouped by Phase4) was about $70,000. Some money was spent on home video trade ads, the Power *headbands (promo item), the LA launch party, screeners, shipping, and the expensive Foil O-card special DVD packaging which did look snazzy in my opinion and was done to help drive retail DVD sales, especially Walmart.*

Did you premiere at a prominent festival?

> **Ari:** *We premiered at Sundance.*

How much did you spend to "open" at the festival—publicists etc.

> **Ari:** *Not much.*

How much did you spend for the marketing and promotion of your release?

> **Ari:** *$150,000 including prints.*

Who did you hire?

> **Ari:** *Press Contact NY: Long Lead / Emma Griffiths PR, Emma Griffiths, (917) 438-5074*
>
> *Press Contact LA: mPRm Public Relations, René Ridinger, (323) 933-3399 x 4271*
>
> *Local markets PR*
>
> *Variance in-house (in other words Ari cold-calling, and this was the only thing that actually worked)*

Did you track your online analytics related to specific promotional activities?

> **Ari:** *They did not.*

Did you purchase any media (print ads, radio or TV, web banner ads)? How much did you spend on each?

> **Anne:** *Jivox—part of the Phase4 budget (as noted above, this cost $15,000)—online, rich media ads which linked to landing pages which I created for our website. This was one of Susan Boyer's initiatives.*

Were the media buys effective?

> **Ari:** *This is absolutely impossible to measure because we couldn't track it effectively. It didn't feel that effective, though.*

Did you purchase Facebook Ads or Google Ads? How much did you spend? Were they effective?

> **Anne/Ari:** *We spent $20,000. Facebook is a tough nut to crack. We have a great fan base—over 100K. We need to learn how to better reach these fans. The ads are highly effective, but it is important to have a clear goal in place when you have someone click on your ad. I look forward*

to the integration of DIY distribution and Facebook. Once we can have the film available for download directly on our Facebook page, I believe we will really be able to harness the power of this social network to its fullest extent. We have a lot of fans in Latin America—territories where Adventure of Power *is not yet available. Making the film available to these fans, right on the FB page is a very exciting, soon-to-be reality.*

It should be noted that Ari and Anne will be working on a DIY strategy for the film with Distrify and Prescreen. I introduced Ari to Prescreen after Prescreen came on board to sponsor this book, long after I selected this film to be a part of it. I had introduced Distrify to Ari as well via my coverage of them in a blog about DIY tools and solutions. More about the DIY plans for the future is covered below.

Did you have any online competitions? Were they effective?

Anne: *Yes. We are doing an* online air-drum battle *right now (we partnered with DrumChannel). The judging of the top ten finalists aired live on Wed., June 15, 2011 at 6pm PST on* DrumChannel.com. *We launched a video on You-Tube which stated the rules, etc., and which was fun content to watch. We milked this competition in every way possible—promoting it on our website, sending out email blasts and we used it as a means to reach out to radio stations for press. Ari did a bunch of interviews about the competition on rock and college radio stations."*

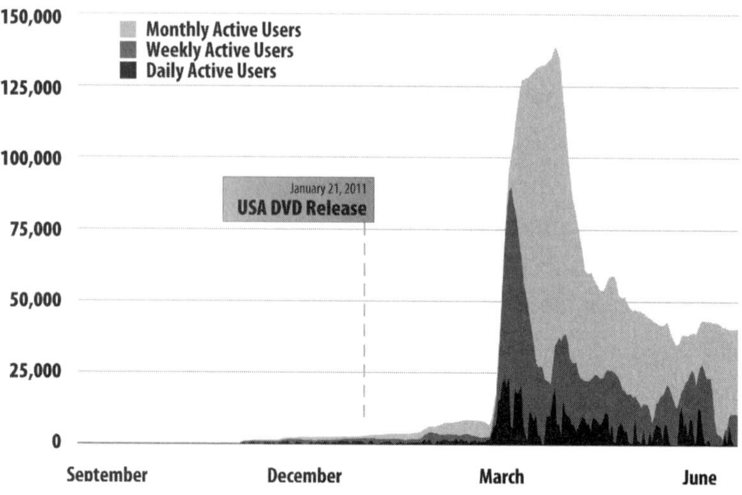

Anne: *A bit more about our radio tour. We kept Susan Boyer on after the launch to help run our press/radio campaign. We felt that 42West hadn't done enough targeted outreach. Susan went through Ari's list of contacts, researched the markets and carefully crafted emails: she stuck to her guns and yielded good results. I wanted to broaden our net and suggested spamming as many radio stations as possible to try to get interviews that way. Susan was categorically against it. I used my copy of "The Musician's Atlas" and generated a spreadsheet with the stations' call letters, name of the DJ, location, etc., and Ari crafted a great email which we sent out to thousands of DJs. We had several interviews every week for a while, and we still have interviews trickling in. This yielded results in big and small markets as well as college radio, which is a great demographic for us. We even got one screening at a school through this spam. I also googled "Adventures of Power" and searched for stations that blogged about Ari (he did a drum-off with Rush drummer Neil Peart and rock radio stations love Peart, so this*

5. PRESENT DISTRIBUTION—DVD, BROADCAST, VOD & DIGITAL—USA/NORTH AMERICA

In 2010 TFC secured a distribution deal with Phase4. Ari did not want to just do DIY. Given the cast, he naturally wanted to get into key retailers and onto key platforms and do a television deal, etc. The filmmakers added over 90 minutes of bonus features and all of them, including the director's commentary, are closed captioned for the deaf and hard of hearing (Ari paid for the captioning out of his own pocket).

DVD SALES—VIA A DISTRIBUTOR

The deal with Phase4 was done long after the film premiered at Sundance. It was not an MG deal (i.e. a deal with a Minimum Guarantee) because we preferred better backend terms in this case, given that getting a high enough MG was no longer an option and Ari had not implemented DIY distribution. Ari had not been selling DVD units himself. Most of the DVD revenue has not yet been collected by Phase4, so it is too soon to tell what that will yield. The DIY that Ari can do is just getting started, so it is too soon to tell on that front as well. Phase4's contract was relatively reasonable and the Term was 7 years, which is somewhat short for traditional distributors. Its distribution fee is standard.

Phase4 used 42 West to handle publicity for the film. Ari noted that very little publicity was generated and that it's generally very hard to get publicity for an indie film if a studio is not behind it.

Getting traditional press coverage for an indie release, with news staffs being slashed, has become increasingly difficult. Even while Ari was touring with the film the movie was not reviewed in most local papers. When the DVD came out, Ari, at the last minute was able to secure interest from Time Magazine, which could have been a coup, but Phase4 did not send a screener out to the magazine in time from Canada.

DVD SALES—UNITS, PACKAGING, REVENUE, EXPENSES, ETC.

Recouped expenses were capped at a five-figure sum plus on-going replication. Phase4 is direct with Walmart, and they created quite lovely packaging and the DVD sold into Walmart. Sadly, the film was too small for Redbox, although they did try. Of course, Blockbuster was over by the time this DVD came out (the DVD street date was January 21, 2011).

Key U.S. retailers/wholesalers carrying the AoP DVD: AEC, Amazon.com, Arrow Distribution, Baker & Taylor, Edge Distribution (college stores), Hastings, Ingram, Flash Distributor (wholesalers), Midwest Tapes, Netflix, Softland, Super D, Waxworks, VPD (sub-distributor for family video).

Canadian retailers/wholesalers carrying the AoP DVD: Blockbuster, eOne (sub-distributor), HMV, Rentrak, Rogers, Videotron/Jumbo Video, Walmart.

Please note that the sub-distributors typically sell into convenience stores, regional video chains and small (fewer than five store fronts) retailers.

DIGITAL RIGHTS—TELEVISION AND CABLE

Cable VOD

It's too soon to get reporting about performance. The film was available on: Comcast, Cablevision, Charter, Time Warner, Brighthouse, Fios. There was some trouble making sure the cast was always listed.

Quarterly accounting did not reflect digital revenue yet, and in fact, very little revenue has come in at the time of this case study.

Phase4 sold the film to Showtime for a respectable, if not extremely high, five-figure fee (it could have been a higher fee if the film had been newer, the theatrical done better, Netflix not been allowed, etc.). With both the Showtime fee and the Netflix SVOD fee we're getting to close to high five-figures. Again, newer films can do better on both the TV money and the Netflix SVOD fee, but I think time took its toll.

"Conventional" Digital Rights—(e.g. Streaming, Download)

Adventures of Power (through Phase4) is available on:

- iTunes
- Amazon On Demand
- Blockbuster On Demand
- CinemaNow
- YouTube Rental
- Netflix SVOD
- Microsoft XBOX
- VUDU (WalMart's digital platform as of 2010, when the retail giant acquired it.)
- Sony Playstation
- Hulu is a free service, so Phase4 wants to exploit all paid avenues before servicing the film to pay free outlets.

6. MERCHANDISING, CORPORATE SPONSORSHIP, PARTNERSHIPS AND DIY DISTRIBUTION

I'd love some info about the merchandising. What was made, for how much, how was it used, and did it work?

Anne: *We have sweatshirts, but I don't think any have sold—they are through a* website, *where you don't pay anything upfront. If someone buys it they make it and ship it, and people will do just about anything for a sweatband, but we are giving them away for free. We also ask Facebook fans to do things, such as translate a page, or put a comment on iTunes, and then we will send them a sweatband.*

Here's Ari promoting those headbands in another email promo:

From: "Ari Gold" <ari@arigoldfilms.com>
Date: July 6, 2011 6:56:19 AM PDT
Subject: headbands are cool.

I think rockstars & tennis players are cool with headbands. Lots of people have been asking for 'em. So: DrumChannel is giving away two AirDrummer headbands with every DVD of my movie that you buy from them. That's pretty rad: get 'em here: http://www.drumchannel.com/store/products/53

Here's me, drummer Cobus, and DWDrums president Don Lombardi sportin' em at the Air Drum Battle:

And me and Fred (Lucas Cruikshank) expressing the joy of headbands:

Wear with pride. Ok!

Ari

Which consultants did you work with?

Anne/Ari: *TFC, Susan Boyer, Believe (YouTube promo), and a sponsorship consultant who shall remain nameless.* [TFC charged its initial membership fee. At the time it was the introductory price of $250, and then we charged another $1,000 for contract consultation (2 contracts) and another $500 for marketing and general extended distribution consultation.]

How effective were they?

Anne/Ari: *The sponsorship consultant was a total waste of money. We paid $1500. She "prepared" a deck for potential sponsorship. She required constant hand-holding, couldn't prepare the deck on her own—didn't know how to use PowerPoint software, etc. The list goes on and on. She was very hard to work with, difficult personality.* [Full disclosure: TFC connected Ari to this person but we did not know she would charge that flat fee. We had a very pleasant working relationship with her and we also thought she would be on commission only and/or a lower consultation fee. Ari wanted to leave her name out of this book.]

Did you get any sponsorship? If so, for what?

Anne: *We got low five-figures from Onitsuka Tiger (Asics Sneakers) for our DVD launch party. Onitsuka Tiger had worked with Ari's band The Honey Brothers a few times in the past and we hit them up directly, through the band's manager.*

PARTNERSHIPS & CAUSES

AoP partnered with VH1's Save the Music.

Can you give us numbers for Save the Music?

> **Ari:** *I think we raised around $21K—but we are now doing round two and hope to raise more. We're going to restore a school's music program.*

What did Save the Music do for the film? Please go into detail about that entire relationship, the deal, and how it came about.

> **Anne:** *Ari insisted from the beginning of the campaign that if you want to hook in publications to get press, you should have a charity event. He had been donating his film for charity screenings and getting press that way for a while. I believe (and Ari does too) that Susan Boyer reached out to VH1. We felt that it was the right organization because they have a lot of press connections and their own press machine. We had to decide whether or not we wanted to guarantee that we could raise a certain amount of money (I think it was $30K). They would get involved with us no matter what, but if we wanted their full support, celebrity involvement, etc., we needed to make that $30K guarantee, which we didn't do. We ended up raising over $20K so far and saved a whole music program. We haven't chosen the school yet, but we will do a giant check presentation, press, etc., probably in the fall. VH1 connected us with charitybuzz, who ran the online auction, coordinated with the item donors and the bidders, dealt with shipping and follow-up, etc.*

Were there any promotional partnerships you did not cover? What did they do for you, and what did you have to do for them?

> **Anne:** *We had screenings for charity to benefit Baltimore Youth Orchestra and United Nations Year of Youth in To-*

ronto. We donated the film and got press in return. There may have been a few other screenings. For the VH1 Save the Music Foundation Auction, we got a lot of the artists who donated to Tweet about the auction, and thus our film.

Please elaborate a tad, and give some more details about how this worked and who did it and what the results were.

Anne: *Every time we get mentioned on Rush's Facebook page we get thousands of hits on our website. Ween mentioned the auction and drummer Claude Coleman's appearance at the live Air Drum Battle finals, and both times this resulted in a spike in visits to our Facebook page and website. We had an amazing list of donors for the auction, including Ringo Starr, Ke$ha, Metallica, Jane Lynch, David Wain, Neil Peart…this list goes on and on. These artists all helped to support our auction and* Adventures of Power.

MERCHANDISE SALES & DIY

When you buy your DVDs from your distributor—how much do you pay per unit?

Anne: *They extended us a special rate of less than $5.00/ unit to use for promotional purposes.*

In my opinion, $5.00 or less is the right price to pay for DVD units from a distributor and that revenue should be factored into the grosses as well. Ari and his team did not sell DVDs or other Merchandise from his sites or at events.

ABOUT AOP'S DIY

What DIY will you be doing in the future?

Anne: *We have launched with Distrify and will do Prescreen. We're excited to reach our fans in Latin America.*

The film isn't available there, so we can set a really competitive price and reach the people.

Speak to how did they connect and work with Adventures of Power?

Andy Green (co-owner of Distrify): *In March 2011 Distrify was just getting started. We'd built our player and had some great features online, but no films really (we had a few of our own and some from friends but nothing from the 'open market.') Programmer Jim Kolmar invited me to SXSW after I Tweeted about the festival. At Distrify we saw this trip as a great way to connect with the sharpest people in the new distribution biz. Among others, I met with Orly Ravid of The Film Collaborative, and this was a really special moment. I've been genuinely inspired by Orly's work and approach, so it was great to meet her in Texas. Later that month Orly introduced Distrify to Ari Gold. I'd seen a post from Ari on Hope for Film and really wanted to work on his film Adventures of Power. Ari emailed me so we got started.*

On Facebook + Distrify client side, Ari works with Anne Bernstein who is the PMD [Producer of Marketing and Distribution] on Power. We immediately laid out what we wanted to do with each other, and for Distrify that involved building some quite complex, new features. For Ari and Anne this involved adding some extra content and improving the delivery. A great job has been done building a Facebook group of 100K+ followers, and Ari was connecting well via Twitter and by doing special events nationwide. By analyzing the social media conversation in context with some broad analytics we realized that a substantial number of deaf people were interested in Power (Shoshanna Stern is one of the main actors) and that around half of the social media group live in Mexico.

In terms of the player/purchase options, Ari noticed a huge emerging fan base in Mexico that he speaks of in his interview. He realized 50% of his 100,000 Facebook fans were in Mexico. Distrify added Spanish closed captions as well as English and they introduced streaming as an option in Mexico. They've been told that several companies prevent streaming in Mexico, and they added the Mexican Peso as a currency that people can sell with.

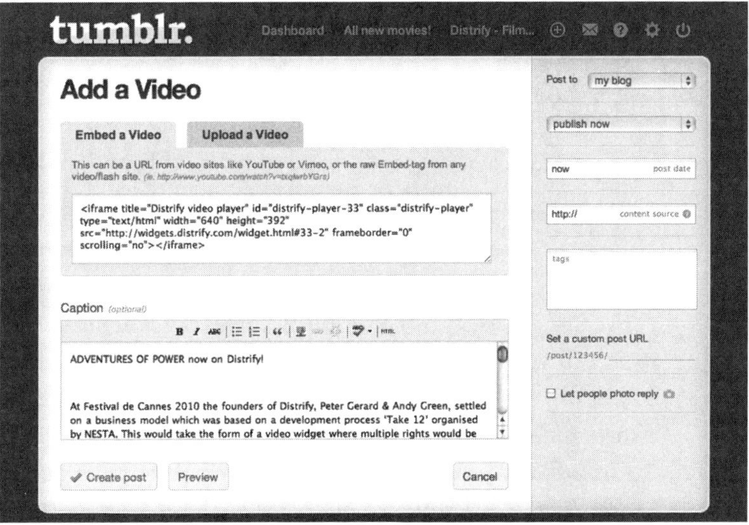

Distrify Embed Tool

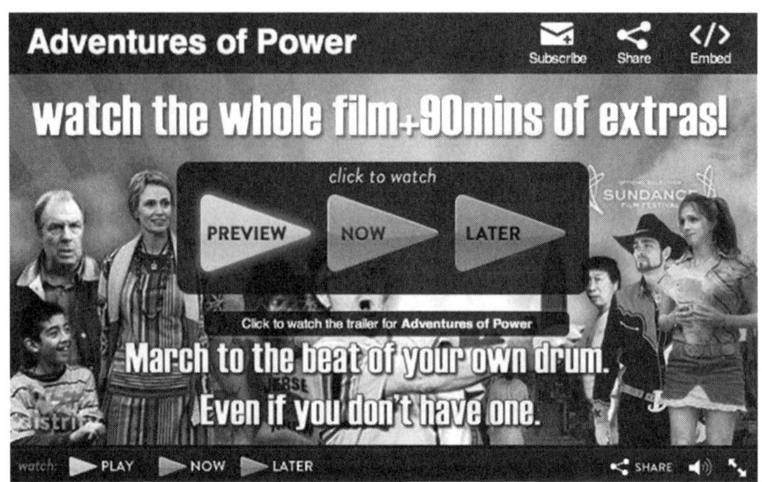

Distrify Preview Screen

This conversation, between filmmaker, audience and distributor is the antithesis of the present way films are most commonly distributed and marketed. Our new way: it's a conversation where a community forms around the niche aspects of a film and then the film reacts to this conversation to improve its offer to the audience. In essence the audience is telling the filmmaker/distributor how to market the film. To secure this valuable interaction, in the long term, needs more than conversation alone. Distrify offers affiliate revenue to audiences with the rate set by the rights-holder, and in the case of Power this is 30% (to start with). The intention is to engender micro-marketing film blogs where reviewers earn real money—we want to see successful business spring up around the revenue-sharing model and in many currencies around the world.

Facilitating new business is of equal importance to a better deal for rights-holders. We truly believe in a revolution, where audiences and filmmakers are directly connected but also share in the profits. This philosophy is shared, we believe, by Adventures of Power; *in many ways this film has the same values and sense of fun!*

7. CONCLUSION

I know that from my point of view, a lot was done well and correctly, but the mistake was in waiting too long and that took its toll.

Have any lessons been learned? Is there anything you would definitely do again and definitely not do again?

Anne: *Oh boy. That is so hard to say. This is me talking, not Ari. I don't know what to say about putting so much money and effort into making and trying to sell a physical DVD. Probably our path will be more through online (digital) at first. I am really excited to see what happens now that we will be on Netflix streaming and on Showtime. Maybe those deals only happened because a DVD deal was in place. It's so hard to calculate this shit.*

The grassroots outreach was great—it took some effort, but limited resources. For example, the radio tour that we booked through spamming; Ari talked to every station that wrote back—big or small. We have connected with some hard-core fans that way. The numbers are really hard to gauge through radio, but it was satisfying.

I am thinking that college campuses, niche blogs, and online should be our main focus. You can expend a lot of energy trying to bag "big" interview ops, but so far little has come from the few we got—such as the Adam Carola interview; not much came of that and it took a shitload of energy to make it happen.

We still have a ton of tricks up our sleeves. We are launching round two of our auction this fall and we have a screening coming up in Madrid in early September where we will show our Spanish subtitled version for the first time to a live

There were great efforts and interesting and useful service partners for the most part, all spearheaded by a wildly creative, energetic
and mindful creator. The efforts started too late and there was no
plan in place for what ultimately happened, which was a changed
market climate at Sundance in 2008 that Ari and so many others
were not prepared for because it was not anticipated. No big sale
was going to just make it all work out and make Ari's dream come
true. Money was lost on the theatrical but that is always a gamble
and had it been timed better with other components of the release it
would have been more useful, e.g. day-and-date Theatrical & VOD.
Coming out on DVD and Digital platforms three years after a festival premiere is not ideal, but Ari is making the most of it and the
campaign is working and his fan base is growing and he's certainly a
great example of how to work DIY and one's own brand.

American: The Bill Hicks Story

By Orly Ravid

American: The Bill Hicks Story,
directed by Paul Thomas and Matt Harlock

I met Paul Thomas and Matt Harlock, the filmmakers of *American: The Bill Hicks Story* at SXSW 2010. They had some distribution company interest stemming from the fest and other DIY/Hybrid option interest, and they and we investigated several options on all fronts, but the right all-rights deals did not present themselves to the filmmakers. Having gone into personal debt to cover the unexpectedly steep animation costs, they opted for a split-rights/hybrid scenario. As Paul Thomas says, "It's the bigger picture that is more interesting, and how the various elements fit together as a strategy, so here's the brief snapshot of that."

Paul Thomas and Matt Harlock: *We've experienced many different models, from different split-right scenarios in the USA & UK to all-rights deals in Australia and rest of world, and we've been on a thorough learning curve over the last couple of years.*

The BBC provided initial production funding through a DVD advance and TV acquisition fee totaling $280,000 (this is a NET #; 20% of the gross fee went to their UK rep). However, this included $60,000 (again, this is a NET # after the fee to the UK rep) for USA DVD rights. It was this that caused the filmmakers problems later. They were not able give any US distributor an all-rights deal, and this ultimately led them to handle the split-rights themselves.

Paul & Matt: *At SXSW we met both Nolan Gallagher from* Gravitas *and Dylan Marchetti from* Variance Films, *who were both very keen to work on the film. Nolan said that a theatrical would help secure strong VOD placement across the platforms and that a day-and-date VOD release with theatrical would work best to achieve this. We did consider releasing with the help of a cheaper theatrical booker, but with one shot to get it right we concluded that Variance would achieve the best that was possible and so decided to run with their larger fee.* [Note: TFC advised on this front as well.]

Dylan got the minimum P&A [Promotions & Advertising] *down to around $23,000, with his fee on top. He took some money up front in a cash budget, and the rest from the box-office proceeds. Dylan preferred we not disclose his fees or budget since they vary depending on the scale of release.* [Note: I reviewed the P&A budget. It was all quite normal lean spending on minimal print ads, street marketing and PR.]

We would like to have launched earlier in the USA but

*had to wait for our Australian advance to come through
and then we missed the fall slots. Variance then suggested
avoiding Oscar season, and coordinated with Gravitas for
a theatrical spring release date of April 8, 2011. Concurrently, Gravitas and Warner Digital Distribtion lined up the
same VOD date. As a result, the film opened in theatres and
was available in 100 million homes via major VOD operators such as Comcast, Time Warner Cable, Dish Network,
AT&T, Verizon, Apple iTunes and Amazon Instant Video.*

*Trailers then worked across both platforms announcing the
day-and-date availability in cinema and home pay-per-
view. So, Dylan has his full fee, and we're currently about
$20K down, when we had expected it would at least break
even. Dylan said that a lot of theaters didn't take it because
of the day-and-date VOD, which we knew was the risk you
take, plus we've also had the Hicks factor of a doc about a
marginal figure for a lot of Americans. However, the theatrical is what led Warner to place it well across all their platforms and aggressively market it on screen in cable homes,
resulting in over 20,000 month-1 sales at the $6.99 price
point* [grossing over $160,000 in the first month].

The filmmakers would "still love to find a way of giving [the
film] a decent television outing." Gravitas got a good Netflix deal,
but they feel there's something about a broadcaster presenting to
their audience that is really important for a significant historical
figure like Hicks."

The DVD came out on June 8, 2011, along with a lower VOD/
iTunes price point, so it will be interesting to see how the sales
curve continues. I will revisit the Gravitas release in more detail
later in the chapter.

The filmmakers also worked on a simultaneous Canadian release with Ryan Levey at Vagrant Films in Toronto, who did a
simple 50/50 deal with no fees for theatrical. Ryan took around

CAD$1,500 in expenses and Canada grossed around CAD$12,000.

> **Paul & Matt:** *The day-and-date theatrical/VOD did affect many cinemas' decisions to take the film, and Variance warned that we might lose several potential theatres with a day-and-date release with VOD.*

> **Variance (Dylan Marchetti):** [Regarding theatres' general willingness to show a film when it's having a day-and-date VOD release…] *Almost all of the chains have taken a hard line against any film with a VOD window of less than 94 days. A significant portion of the independent theaters have decided that for the right film, it doesn't really hit them in the pocketbook and they'll tolerate it (supporting it is a stretch), as long as you present them with a fleshed-out plan as to why people will come to the theater rather than simply stay at home.*

Of course, the film found its theatrical homes. With their small P&A they still achieved a $7,000 opening weekend at Cinema Village in NY and reached a total USA gross of $90,589, though they failed to break even. Click here for the box-office gross report for the first four weeks of the release, which also lists the theatres the film played during this time period.

> **Paul & Matt:** *The theatrical release secured a lot of favorable film press and allowed Gravitas to present a strong case to Warner, who gave the film great placement across their VOD and PPV networks at a $6.99 premium price point. The film stayed on iTunes' top 10 documentaries for two months and performed well across the States. Gravitas estimated it grossed $160,000 that first month, and that it will reach $600,000 gross over the next 3 years. Without the theatrical lead, it's unlikely we would get anywhere near that figure.*

KEY PRESS QUOTES

★★★★
"Nothing short of astounding"
TIME OUT

★★★★
"Extraordinary—a triumph of style and content…"
UNCUT

"A brilliant and beguiling film—a fitting tribute to one
of comedy's all-time greats."
ESQUIRE

★★★★
"This inventively constructed, dynamically executed
documentary will make you laugh a lot, but more
importantly, it'll make you wanna get off you arse
and DO SOMETHING."
BIZARRE

"I just loved it, I sat there with a huge grin on my face
the whole time. Really innovative. It needs to be seen."
Richard Linklater

Paul & Matt: *We're still looking for a US TV deal, but there were no instant takers. VOD clearly causes tension for the US broadcasters, while UK broadcasters are more relaxed about it. The commercial logic here is that a strong VOD performance reveals a large TV audience for the broadcasters since VOD numbers are actually tiny relative to broadcast audience. In the US we got a strong Netflix deal based on the early VOD numbers, and perhaps it's only a matter of time before broadcasters realize the usefulness of VOD too as the two platforms find ways to work together.*

Beyond the UK & North America, we did a $30K all-rights deal with Madman Australia, who achieved a 78k gross against a spend of $1,700. Melbourne's ACMI cinema *grossed $40K by itself, demonstrating that there are clearly pockets of untapped audience who respond well when a venue knows how to reach and motivate that audience. Who knows how much of a wider audience is waiting in every region but aren't fully in touch with what's happening in their art house theatres. We repeatedly heard from people on Facebook & Twitter who had missed the film in their region. That's where there's huge potential for an app, where you register your interest on download, and then automatic screening reminders are sent based on your location, as the film reaches theaters.*

Internationally, the rest of world sales are pretty poor. Autlook Films came on board shortly before we released our UK DVD, having initially said "This is a great film for the whole world," and seeming very positive. However, they cautioned us that online downloads ripped from the UK DVD might affect sales and, whether this is the reason or not, the real picture several months later is that we've had no significant international sales and just two small TV acquisitions from Finland and Israel.

One thing we wish we'd been more aware of is the way some sales agents will handle your film. Autlook pretty much refused to communicate information outside of six monthly sales reports, which we're currently waiting on, so we have no clear picture of the detail of what they have tried or where interest has or hasn't existed. This has been very frustrating compared with the open communication with our Stateside partners for VOD, Theatrical, DVD and press, where the mix & match team worked brilliantly together to coordinate the best release for the film vs. market conditions. We know of plenty of other filmmakers who are having the same experience—with decisions about where their film will play taken out of their hands, and very little feedback about progress or ongoing strategy. For some filmmakers, this works—just finishing your film, handing it over to someone else and moving on but, for us, connecting this film with audiences has continued to be important, and the openness and swift communication from everyone on US teams has fitted perfectly with our own aims and our closeness to the underlying aims of the project.

The industry is in huge flux, and until things have settled into a clearer set of practices and revenue splits, the hybrid approach of negotiating the separate rights placements with the most appropriate individual distributors and aggregators has been by far the better approach for us. The difference is definitely something everyone should be aware of.

The above covers the core narrative of this film's distribution. Below are some detailed answers to questions in the various distribution and marketing categories so you, gentle reader, can isolate more specifics.

DISTRIBUTION SALES

SALES REPS

Did you have a domestic sales rep? If so who?

Paul & Matt: *No Domestic sales rep although we used a producer's rep to assist in coordinating our UK funding through combined UK & USA DVD advance (discussed above) and BBC UK TV acquisition, leaving us with all other world rights. We then approached many UK film sales reps, but our US DVD rights had already gone and the reps were all looking for world rights.*

Do you have a foreign sales rep? If so who?

Paul & Matt: *Autlook films based in Austria.*

Did you find them effective?

Paul & Matt: *Autlook have secured some B-tier festival screenings, but other world sales are almost non-existent. We found Autlook several months after our US premier, and our UK DVD release date was already in place, which affected the foreign sales Autlook could secure. Rather than seeing the online illegal download audience as a useful measure of the total audience potential, European broadcasters instead think illegal downloads poach a large part of their audience and we have no significant TV sales. Again, it's an area where UK broadcasters are more relaxed about the true size of the home audience and the way those mainstream TV audiences behave compared with online audiences.*

What is your deal with them?

Paul & Matt: *Autlook takes 35% with expenses capped at €5,000.*

How many consultants did you work with (name them)?

Paul & Matt: *We took some initial advice from Jon Reiss after meeting him at Sundance and also worked with Orly Ravid at The Film Collaborative.*

How effective were they?

Paul & Matt: *Jon provided great advice and some introductions, which is really important when you are working without an exec producer. Orly gave us a great deal of time, stemming from our complicated US rights situation, and outlined both the US landscape for us and the potential shape of some deals. From both of them we had very valu-*

able discussions working through the kind of deals we did and didn't want. Orly also put in several calls to US channels and distributors for us, but ultimately, none of these outlets wanted the film so we went down the route of self-funding the theatrical and working with Gravitas on the VOD, which all worked out very successfully.

How much did you spend on consultants?

Paul & Matt: *$700.* [They joined TFC at the $350 level.]

FOREIGN SALES

Were there any overall sales outside the US?

Paul & Matt: *UK—$225K for DVD, $67.5K for UKTV, $7.5K for UK audio-only release. We are still waiting for the UK VOD figures.*

Are there any Foreign TV sales only—and how much?

Paul & Matt: *Our rest of world TV sales have so far reached just over $8K.*

LIVE EVENT THEATRICAL

FILM FESTIVALS

The film played at the London Film Festival and SXSW in the USA. The filmmakers spent $3,600 on LFF UK press and $5,000 on publicists for SXSW to "open" at the festival—publicists etc. (They worked with MPRM in the US.)

Other than your Festival premiere, what was your strategy around Film Festivals in general? Did you play many or just a few, and why or why not?

> **Paul & Matt:** *Our key aim with the film was to spread awareness of Bill Hicks' story and so we chose to go quite wide with our festival strategy. Overall, the festival strategy worked well; we played around 40 festivals and the film was well placed on Friday/Saturday night slots and most screenings were full.*

Did you charge the Festivals screening fees to show your film? If so, how much did you gross?

> **Paul & Matt:** *We enquired about screening fees, but didn't receive any from any festival. Our international sales agent, Autlook Films, successfully charged for the screenings they have handled. We could have been more bullish with our requests for fees, especially as several festivals did extremely well with our film, but because of the strong responsibility we felt to Bill's story and the need to make sure people heard of the film and got to know his work, we didn't want to risk losing the screening slots. Ultimately, knowing that smaller festivals baulk at even $250 screening fees means we might have lost out on a potential $5,000-$10,000 at the larger festivals we played, but in the overall scheme of things that is less significant than developing an audience for the film."* The filmmakers also noted this was new to them and they felt unsure of themselves with respect to charging festivals, which we encounter quite often with filmmakers.

festival	notes
BFI London Film Festival	World Premiere
SXSW Film Festival	US Premiere
Sheffield International Documentary Festival	
Dublin International Film Festival	
Glasgow International Film Festival	
Belfast International Film Festival	
True/False Film Festival, Columbia, MO	prestigious 'Secret Screening' slot
Dallas International Film festival	won *MPS Filmmaking Award*
Independent Film Festival Boston	
HotDocs: Canadian International Documentary Festival, Toronto	
Little Rock Film Festival	won *Texas Filmmakers Award*
Seattle International Film Festival	
Just For Laughs Film Festival, Montreal	
Indianapolis Film Festival	
Edmonton International Film Festival	
Branchage Film Festival, Jersey	
Downtown Los Angeles Film Festival	won *Best Documentary* award
Friars Comedy Festival New York	
Bologna Biografilm Festival	won *Best documentary* award

Festivals at which the film has played

Outside of the Festival circuit, did you hold community-based word-of-mouth/buzz screenings? Did you feel they were helpful? Do you have any way to empirically back that up?

Paul & Matt: *We explored this in London for our theatrical and DVD launch, but due to the organizational load required, we didn't pursue it. However, the film's subject, Bill Hicks, would have been 50 years old this year, so we may explore some celebration screenings to mark that date.*

CONVENTIONAL THEATRICAL

Did you do traditional theatrical, and if so, how much time did you spend to set it up?

> **Paul & Matt:** *We did theatrical runs in the UK, Australia, Canada and the USA. We realized early on that we had a strong theatrical film, which was a mixed blessing as we then had to spend several years animating to make sure we hit its full potential. Thankfully, this was confirmed with an amazing response at the London Film Festival screenings. We felt strongly that the film was an 'audience film,' and that because of the subject matter (stand-up comedy), and what Bill's work was trying to achieve, it was really important for people to be able to experience the film in that way. Theatrical is also the only way that most newspapers will review the film, which is an important consideration when operating with very small advertising budgets.*

The UK was handled by our DVD distributor 2Entertain (the home entertainment arm of the BBC). The film went on to become the 2nd highest grossing documentary released theatrically in the UK in 2010. This meant that the theatrical came close to breaking even, but is still essentially a publicity-generating device. The USA theatrical took around a year to establish, but this was largely due to our own time constraints and needing to wait until we had the available cash-flow to fund it. Madman took Australian rights and mounted a very successful theatrical run there.

How much did you spend on the theatrical?

> **Paul & Matt:** *The UK theatrical cost $90K and the US theatrical cost significantly less. Meanwhile, Madman spend just a few thousand to secure several prominent screenings and achieved $78K gross there in a handful of well picked screens.*

Did you use a service company?

> **Paul & Matt:** *Yes, Verve Pictures in the UK and Variance Films in the USA.*

How long was the theatrical run?

> **Paul & Matt:** *The UK theatrical ran for 12 weeks and played 21 screens as full week+ runs, and another 31 venues as short runs. The USA has run for 11 weeks to date and played full week+ runs in 17 cities with shorter runs in another 11 venues and more that will occur post the date of this book being finalized (July 2011).*

How much did you GROSS and NET? Can you give a specific on your highest grossing week-long run and lowest grossing week-long run?

> **Paul & Matt:** *UK gross was $180K and the net went back to the distributor. USA gross is $79K with net still to be calculated.*

> **Variance (Dylan Marchetti):** *There's some of the collateral we created, along with a general list of the in-theater events we had in NYC and LA on opening weekend (we did events in nearly every market, whether it be a comedian doing a 5-minute "warm-up" set before the film, or someone who knew Bill coming in for an intro/Q&A, or just a simple Skype Q&A with Matt and Paul for the markets they weren't there to open themselves).*

> *We also had great success and a spike in web traffic when we debuted the trailer exclusively on Apple iTunes trailers (with a "page topper," though I don't have a screenshot) and the poster at Gordon and the Whale, a Texas-based film site that got us a lot of play down there.*

Sample theatrical ads. Note that the VOD is even tagged.

ALTERNATIVE THEATRICAL (INCLUDES NON-, SEMI- AND COMMUNITY THEATRICAL)

In how many cities did you have alternative theatrical screenings?

Paul & Matt: *Due to the conventional theatrical release and our bookers relationship with those theaters, we didn't feel we could also set up community screenings, but may explore this for other significant dates coming up. Variance* *has booked a handful of these (at least for as of the time of this being written in July) and most come with flat screening fees ad the theatres keep the door.*

MERCHANDISE SALES

DVD SALES—VIA A DISTRIBUTOR

How many DVD units did you sell via a distributor?

Paul & Matt: *UK has sold around 30K units and we've only just launched in the USA. Warner Home Entertainment handles the BBC's output in the States and have placed the DVD with all the major US outlets and high-street retailers. The DVD is a 2 disk set with 5 hours of extras, which we spent a long time crafting to make sure we really created a compelling reason for people to want to own it vs.. down-loading; the DVD reviews outshone the theatrical reviews.*

How much did you receive from the DVD distributor? Are you still owed money?

Paul & Matt: *The UK & USA DVD advance was $240K, and we receive a further percentage once it breaks even.*

What are your terms with the distributor?

Paul & Matt: *The DVD deal is initially 7 years.*

You buy your DVDs from your distributor...how much do you pay per unit?

Paul & Matt: *Everyone has agreed that we can make digital and physical sales from the website, and the distributor provided some free stock to begin sales. We would then pay around $3 per disk, but haven't put in the mechanisms to start selling them yet.*

What has been your overall experience with your DVD distributor?

Paul & Matt: *Both 2Ent in the UK and Madman in the USA are great teams and responsive, however, they're large companies and so the onus is on the filmmaker to maintain contact and to keep asking questions about how things are going. We also had a deep understanding of what the DVD needed to be for the audience, and so spent considerable time (approx 5 months) cutting 5 plus hours of extras. Fortunately, 2Ent were open to the 2 disk set we felt necessary. We were also lucky to have graphic design experience, and worked closely with both companies in driving and delivering the design for the DVD packaging and theatrical artwork. We produced the graphical menus ourselves, so worked closely with the authoring companies to do this. Maintaining control of all these aspects was very time consuming, but we were glad to have distributors who saw the benefit of the improved package.*

DVD AND OTHER MERCHANDISE SALES FROM YOUR WEBSITE OR AT EVENTS

Which fulfillment company do you use, or do you self-fulfill?

Paul & Matt: *We're just starting to look into this! Because of who Bill was (a very strong, anti-corporate, anti-marketing personality), we had to tread this line extremely carefully, including rights issues with contributors. We do some downloads through TopSpin, who also do merchandise fulfillment but haven't gotten that far yet. We do streaming downloads via Dynamo Player which is working well, but we're also looking at Distrify, who have a referrals system, and we think that motivating the audience to spread awareness of films they like is the way to move forward.*

How much have you made from your own DVD sales?

Paul & Matt: *Nothing yet, due to the advance.*

How much have you made from other merchandise?

Paul & Matt: *Nothing yet; we took 100 t-shirts on our US theatrical tour and gave them all away.*

DIGITAL RIGHTS

TELEVISION AND CABLE

Do you have a US TV deal? If so, on what platform?

Paul & Matt: *We don't have a USA TV deal yet.*

How many Cable VOD platforms are you on?

Paul & Matt: *We're on pretty much everything in the USA, including Time Warner, Comcast, CinemaNow, AT&T, Dish, Verizon, DirectTV, Cox, Charter, SuddenLink and RCN.) Getting on Dish Network's Pay Per View offering was* *a coup for Gravitas, as they usually only take $10M plus performing Hollywood theatrical—this was maybe a result of the theatrical reviews and awareness.*

Gravitas (Nolan Gallagher): *Gravitas Ventures licensed the film after seeing it at SXSW. Gravitas and the filmmakers conceived of the innovative day-and-date strategy and collaborated with Warner Bros. Digital Distribution on the marketing and distribution. American: The Bill Hicks Story was distributed in April 2011 to over 100 cable, satellite, and telco operators, including all major operators such as Comcast, Time Warner Cable, Cox, Charter, Cablevision, Verizon and AT&T. The combined cable and digital VOD release means the film was available in over 100 million North American homes.*

What was unique about the cable VOD release of the film was that it debuted "day-and-date," or at the same time as the theatrical release of the film, so while the documentary was playing in 22 markets to rave reviews, every home with a cable or Internet connection in the United States and Canada could enjoy the film. Because of this unique strategy, many operators carried the film for more than six months."

Do you have a VOD aggregator? If so, who is it?

Paul & Matt: *Gravitas handled the USA VOD for us and have done an amazing job. They are documentary specialists, and have pioneered the reclassifying of docs into its own specialization, which many cable operators had not considered. They also recommend that your film title starts with the letters A-D! This is because success in the VOD market has a lot to do with placement and exposure within the portals that people use to purchase and view content.*

How much money have you made from VOD?

Paul & Matt: *Gravitas are predicting around 600K VOD gross over three years, over half of which will come back to us. The online campaign has been helped by strong reviews and the awareness generated through the theatrical campaign and press, (which we supported with a month long tour of the States.) This led directly to things like additional free banner ads on iTunes, and free 30 second spots on the Dish Network, as these providers saw the initial response and got behind the film.*

Gravitas (Nolan Gallagher): *The early results are very positive, but since the film just came out in April 2011, it will take a few more quarters of consumer activity to get a full financial picture. Combining cable VOD and digital, we estimate about 50,000 consumers will rent the film. Also, thousands of Bill Hicks fans will want to own the film and purchase the EST (electronic sell through) version at a $10-$15 price point. Over the course of the first 3 years, when you add up the ongoing transactional cable and digital VOD, SVOD (i.e. Netflix, Hulu Plus, Amazon Prime, others) and Ad Sponsored VOD (Hulu, others), the filmmakers will likely receive royalties in the multiple six figures.*

"CONVENTIONAL" DIGITAL RIGHTS— (E.G. STREAMING, DOWNLOAD)

American: The Bill Hicks Story was distributed in April 2011 to major digital platforms, including Apple iTunes, Amazon Instant Video, Blockbuster.com, CinemaNow, Sony PlayStation, Microsoft Zune and Vudu. The film was in the top 10 for docs for 7 weeks on iTunes.

Gravitas (Nolan Gallagher): *Gravitas Ventures collaborated with Warner Bros. Digital Distribution on the digital marketing and distribution. The film will play on each platform for years, and Gravitas and Warner will continue* *to 'merchandize' the content on each storefront. Merchandizing could be adding American: The Bill Hicks Story to certain promotional areas (a stand up comedian spotlight section), or engaging in different pricing strategies to generate new interest in the title.*

How much money have you made via any and all digital distribution?

Paul & Matt: *We don't have individual breakdowns yet. Netflix was $xx,xxx* [they disclosed the high-5-figure number but we cannot print it in honor of their contractual obligations]. [Note: these days Netflix is following its internal algorithm more and more and not basing fees on comparable titles but rather on internal stats regarding consumer demand and interaction with a title.]

Gravitas (Nolan Gallagher): *The early results are very positive, but since the film just came out in April 2011, it will take a few more quarters of consumer activity to get a full financial picture.* [See above for their estimates.]

Has there been any APP distribution?

Paul & Matt: *We think an App could have worked very well in our case to reach out to the existing audience and act as a reminder for when the film was coming to their area, but we didn't find a way to create it in time.*

MARKETING DONE BY VOD DISTRIBUTORS

CABLE VOD

Gravitas (Nolan Gallagher): *Cable operators realize that their customers like seeing films like American: The Bill Hicks Story on-demand at the same time that a movie is in theatres. Thus, many cable operators utilized the following impactful marketing tactics to raise the profile of the film within a VOD storefront:*

- ***Barker Videos:*** *Warner Bros. Digital Distribution collaborated with Comcast, the largest operator in North America, to program a 1-minute trailer of American: The Bill Hicks Story in their "barker" video, which plays while their 16 million+ digital customers are deciding what to watch On Demand. Having such a powerful visual reminder of the film at the point of purchase had a tremendous impact on the overall buys of the film.*

- ***VOD Guide Placements:*** *Numerous cable operators placed American: The Bill Hicks Story in some of the most highly consumer trafficked VOD folders, such as "Now in Theatres," "New Release" and "New This Week."*

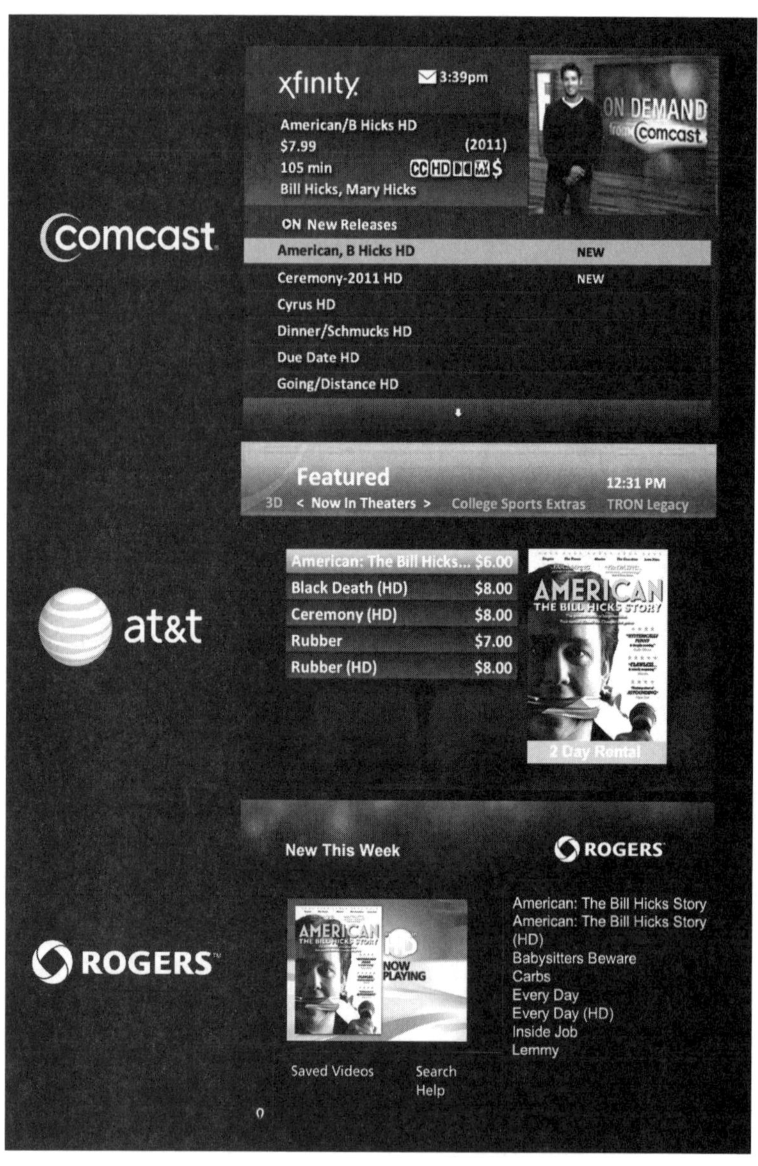

Listings of American: The Bill Hicks Story *on
top Cable VOD platforms*

The fact that iTunes placed American: The Bill Hicks Story *in such sections in the iTunes Store as "New and Noteworthy" and "Stand-Up Comedy" contributed to its landing #2 ranking in the "Top Documentary" section.*

DIGITAL VOD

Gravitas (Nolan Gallagher): *Digital operators like Apple iTunes were also helpful in promoting American: The Bill Hicks Story. They placed the film in high visibility areas within the iTunes storefront, such as "Movies (Main Page),"*

American: The Bill Hicks Story **169**

"New Releases," "New & Noteworthy: Comedy," "New & Noteworthy: Documentary" and "Stand-Up Spotlight." This in-store merchandizing was instrumental in the film becoming the #2 most popular documentary, at one point, behind only the Academy Award winning film, The Inside Job.

MARKETING

PROMOTION AND SOCIAL MEDIA

How much did you spend for the marketing and promotion of your release?

> **Paul & Matt:** *In the UK, our distributor spent approximately $18K overall on traditional PR, another $7K with online agencies handling press and running competitions. One could argue that the theatrical release itself was seen as a marketing expense.*

How much did you spend on publicists? Please separate National, NY, LA, Regional, Affinity?

> **Paul & Matt:** *UK total on PR was approximately $25K. US total was between $10-12K for NY and LA, although these prices were negotiated with people we had worked with before who liked and wanted to help the film.*

> **Variance (Dylan Marchetti):** *Actually, I'm showing $7k total PR for NYC and LA.*

Whom did you hire?

> **Paul & Matt:** *Sarah Wilby Creative Publicity in the UK, an excellent outfit who specialize in high- profile festivals*

and theatrical. We also used MPRM associates in LA (who handled Brokeback Mountain, An Inconvenient Truth and March of the Penguins, all the Coen brothers movies), and Emma Griffiths, a top UK PR in NYC.

How much did you spend on social media? How many months? How much per month? Whom did you hire?

Paul & Matt: *Online agencies in the UK—$7K approximately. USA online was run by Variance (as part of their fee) and us. We also spent some money on Facebook ads for the UK release, but found these difficult to quantify regarding effectiveness. Online is a huge task, and we would have employed someone had we had the funds and found the right person, although we suspect that ongoing payment for this task for most independent films will be a tough issue.*

Did you find your publicists or social media people effective?

Paul & Matt: *Yes. We think that the PR spend we committed to was absolutely necessary when operating without advertising budgets. In markets where we were not on hand to drive press interest, there was a marked dip in the theatrical take.*

Did you track your online analytics related to specific promotional activities?

Paul & Matt: *We didn't track individual campaigns. We saw very visible analytics responses to the combined print & online activities.*

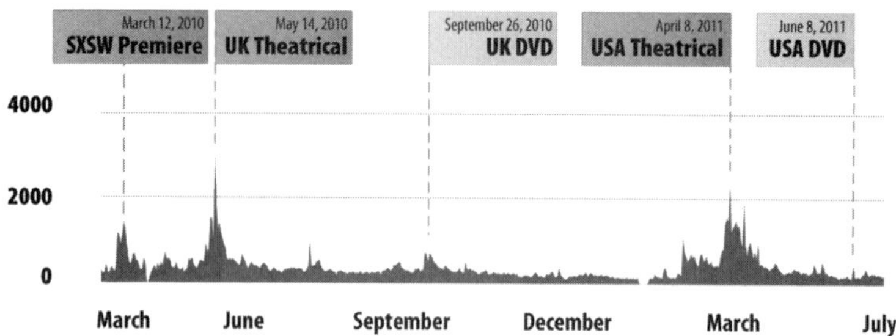

The Google Analytics report above tracks the web hits timeline from SXSW 2010 to date. SXSW was a big initial burst followed by our UK theatrical in May 2010 and US theatrical in April 2011. By comparison to theatrical press and website response, the two DVD release dates—September 26, 2010 and June 8, 2011—are very small bumps. A closer look at March 9, 2011 when the trailer went live on iTunes trailers, the increase in traffic is clearly visible and remains, whereas many website releases just provide a day or two of extra traffic.

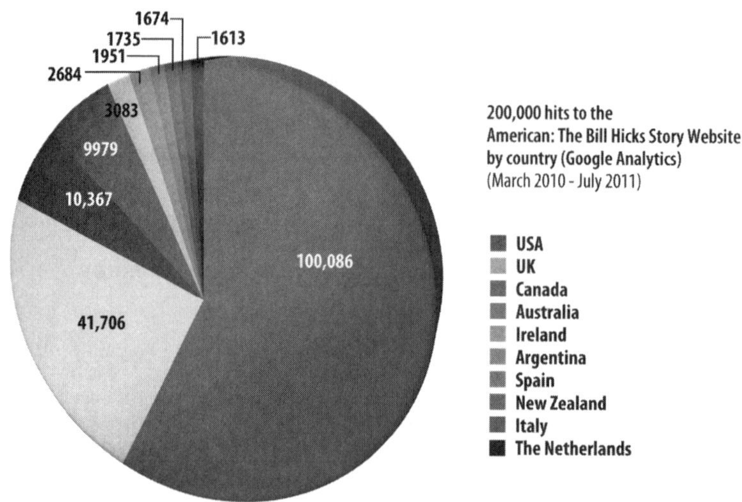

200,000 hits broken down by country, showing the much larger US market even for a UK-centric subject.

This is the opportunity that all the US distributors missed, even though we had seen the vastly larger traffic in UK/ US web hits since our site first launched. In hindsight, we're happy with our hybrid VOD route, but still wonder what audience major US distributor could have realized. We're now seeing a huge Netflix response via twitter (larger than any other release platform by far) but this is STILL just a fraction of the available US audience and we're very aware that most people have still never heard of the film.

The most effective weapon we had in online outreach was content, which is offered as an exclusive to garner prime placement on certain homepages or newsfeeds. This might be in the form of clips, outtakes, audience reactions, new trailers, or famous fans talking about the film. These clips can be time-consuming to create, but are worth doing when the organization in question will hit mailing lists (many we hit were 20,000+), and then support again with a giveaway come the DVD release. These relationships with 'friendly' media need to be created at festivals and then maintained throughout the course of the release.

Did sales increase by any specific promotional activities?

Paul & Matt: *Our site, americanthemovie.com generally receives 400 hits per day, but that escalated to 2,000 per day during our US festival premiere at SXSW, and that figure tended to be matched during other PR pushes.*

Did you purchase any media (print ads, radio or TV, web banner ads)? How much did you spend on each?

Paul & Matt: *For the US release we took out small ads via Variance in NY, LA, Austin and other selected markets. Sometimes these were a requirement of the cinemas we were playing. I should say that outside of NYC and LA, we* *focused ad buys on Internet and Facebook, and only print where required by the theater.*

Were the media buys effective?

Paul & Matt: *It's hard to judge the effectiveness vs. the PR we were doing. We felt on the whole that advertising money was more effectively spent on radio and online outreach, where radio hosts talk enthusiastically about Bill and the film over a longer period and endorse it themselves, and online journos re-post reviews. Cinemas in the major US cities expect there to be press advertising in the local newspapers, and so this is just a requirement you have to accept.*

Did you purchase Facebook Ads or Google Ads? How much did you spend? Were they effective?

Paul & Matt: *A small budget line was attributed to this in the US—approximately $500. We also spent around $750 on Facebook ads in the UK to publicise the DVD release.*

Variance (Dylan Marchetti): *Click-through from Hicks fans was excellent, and roughly 10x typical Facebook ad click-through.*

Do you have any YouTube stats? What activity led to more views?

Paul & Matt: *Our trailers on YouTube have reached over 307,000 views combined with the main trailer, topping 235,000 views. The YouTube channel (AmericanBillHicks) now has nearly 30 video clips, including trailers, audience reactions, making of's, festival Q&A's plus some clips of the film that were previously used to drive online exclusives with sites like GATW, AICN and other supporters of the* *film. Driving views has to do with placement on sites/shows that already have communities who will be interested in your content—film websites, comedy sites in our case, plus radio hosts who have seen the film or who are fans of Bill's work.*

Did you do any online competitions? Were they effective?

Paul & Matt: *We ran online ticket giveaways for the US theatrical release in most markets, and hooked up with local papers, radio stations, comedy clubs or organizations to do the outreach for this. We estimate that we connected with 20-30 different organizations, many of which had 20K+ mailing lists, reaching a total of 200-300K people directly at no cost to us.*

Did you push any other form of content on the web, e.g. video content? How did you do this? Did you pay for this? Did it help your statistics—#s or $s?

Paul & Matt: *See our answer re: YouTube above. We did not pay for any online content placement. iTunes offered us banner ads for free. Everyone else we offered tickets or DVD's as comp prizes/giveaways; we felt this to be extremely effective, but it is based on having had the film play at certain levels of festival and garnering reviews and journalist fans of the film.*

Did you enlist the help of Grassroots Organizations to help promote your film? If so, did they promote the Festival screenings, the theatrical screenings, the DVD release, the Digital Platforms...or what? Do you think their promotion was successful for your bottom line?

> **Paul & Matt:** *We would have liked to do more of these, but the financial mechanisms weren't in place and cinemas would have objected to private screenings during the theatrical. We are however, considering this for the ongoing DVD/VOD campaign.*

> **Variance (Dylan Marchetti):** *I'm not sure I agree with your answer here—I think both you guys and we reached out to TONS of grassroots organizations; we used them to promote theatrical and VOD on the film...I see we've gotten a hold of at least 50-100 in the form of trades or just free promos.*

The filmmakers did not seem to develop financial relationships with Grassroots Organizations to either sponsor the film or help them monetize screenings as that was not quite the right fit for this film.

MORE ABOUT THE MONEY AKA SHOW ME THE MONEY:

Did you raise money for the distribution? If so how much?

> **Paul & Matt:** *We used our Australian advance of $30K to fund the USA distribution. This meant there was a cash flow delay before we could mount the US release.*

How much of the budget was equity investment (to be paid back)?

> **Paul & Matt:** *We provided the debt funding ourselves, and forwent salaries, but due to the very long animation period, this is a large amount that we are unlikely to get back.*

How much money in the budget was from grants, sponsorship, bartering?

> **Paul & Matt:** *Bartering—via deferred salaries, negotiating lower deals with helpful parties, providing services ourselves that would normally have to be line items (e.g. graphic design, PR outreach, etc). Should there be more here?*

Regarding investors: who invested what?

> **Paul & Matt:** *All of this was outlined above regarding 2Entertain and the BBC.*

Have investors been paid back?

> **Paul & Matt:** *The investors are essentially the producers, who have spent almost 5 years on the project without salary and have made a huge cash flow investment. We may be lucky and recoup that actual hard cash, but will be unlikely to take salaries for the time invested.*

Have the below the line crew been paid?

Paul & Matt: **All freelance hires were paid as we went along. Has the director and cast been paid?**

> **Paul & Matt:** *As above, they were paid as filming progressed.*

American: The Bill Hicks Story **177**

Have there been any other sources of revenue?

Paul & Matt: *Yes…prize money! The film won four festivals, LA Downtown, Dallas, Little Rock and Biografilm in Bologna Italy. We received $20K in total prize money, which was a very welcome addition.*

Have any other deals such as remake right sales come out of the film's exhibition?

Paul & Matt: *We have a potential book deal with a UK company that may still happen. In terms of future automated/DIY distribution the filmmakers are working with Top-Spin for downloads and Dynamo for streaming, but neither are currently visible on the website from the US. Matt and Paul note that it is useful to be able to target website sales by country.*

CLOSING TIDBITS AND STATS

- **UK theatrical:** *American: The Bill Hicks Story* is now the 3rd most successful theatrical doc released in the UK this year (2011), outgrossing *It Might get Loud, Tyson, Yes Men,* Oscar-nominees *Burma VJ, Mugabe and The White African,* Oscar-winner *The Cove, FOOD Inc. and Religulous,* and equaling *Capitalism; A Love Story.*

- **iTunes (USA):** *American: The Bill Hicks Story* was one of the Top Ten docs on iTunes for 4+ weeks!

- **Facebook:** *Bill's* various Facebook groups have over 80,000 fans.

- **Website:** The filmmakers' own personal groups/pages for the film have nearly 10,000 members.

- **YouTube:** Their official YouTube trailer now has 120,000 views. Several of Bill's YouTube clips have 1.5 million views.

- List of comedians/filmakers who have seen and actively supported the film:

  > Colin Hanks
  > Jamie Kilstein
  > Paul Provenza
  > Richard Linklater
  > Keith Olbermann

- Comedians who publicly acknowledge Bill Hicks as an inspiration:

  > Kevin Smith
  > Jay Roach
  > Judd Apatow
  > Sarah Silverman
  > Russell Brand
  > Eddie Izzard
  > John Stewart
  > Keith Olberman
  > Larry Charles
  > Mike Judge—Austin
  > Morgan Spurlock
  > Stephen Colbert
  > Bill Maher
  > Noel Fielding

How do Niche Films find their Audiences?

By Jeffrey Winter & Orly Ravid

Niche: "A distinct segment of the market." (dictionary.com)

In today's increasingly fractured media universe, a "niche" is the sweet spot where a film finds a receptive (and oft-times hungry) audience, specifically because it addresses a segment of the market that is replete with vociferous consumers, or a segment of society that is under-represented and eager to see itself reflected onscreen.

Niches of course can be identified by many parameters, be they ethnic, gender-based, age-based, language, lifestyle, community, or identity. Traditionally large niches…such as "women," "teen-aged boys," "fanboys of genre fare such as sci-fi and horror," "men between the ages of 18 and 49," "African-Americans (think Tyler Perry)," right-wing Christians (think *The Passion of The Christ* or the *Narnia* series—actually a rare combination of children, Christians, and genre fanboys)…in fact drive Studio Hollywood business as we know it today.

As we all know, the era of the idea that a piece of filmed content might be for "everyone" is largely dead. There are no more Walter Cronkite newscasts or M.A.S.H finales to drive the majority of the U.S. population to one broadcast station or one viewer experience, (with the possible exception of the Superbowl). Nonetheless, the studio model continues to be one which seeks millions of viewers, and the usual driver in this model is either large movie star casts (declining in relevance every day), or action genres that draw audiences that are simply looking for low-brow escapism based on existing (usually comic book) franchises.

However, for today's independent filmmakers there are a myriad of more subtle niches, many of which are too small to satisfy the wide-release strategies of major distributors, yet which are large enough to prove very successful (and profitable) for films looking to find a particular audience. Major examples in recent years of niches that have been plumbed for their indie potential in the U.S. include "Spanish-language," "environmental-themed," "human rights," "Jewish," "Indian sub-continent/Indian Diaspora," etc. The track-records for these releases have been checkered at best, with at least as many failures as successes recorded to date.

Of all these niches, one that has emerged as relatively easy to identify, market, and distribute to—and relatively stable by comparison to many others – has been the "queer" niche, or what is more politely referred to as "gay and lesbian cinema" or "LGBT film." While the basic dynamics driving LGBT viewers toward LGBT film are not that different from any other niche's desire to see its issues onscreen, queer films have perhaps wrapped themselves even deeper in the "niche" distribution world than most others. This may be because (1) LGBT images have faced particular marginalization in the wider film world, or (2) these films are seen as more "taboo" for crossover audiences, or (3) perhaps their distribution methods have stuck more successfully to the ghettoes than other films. Certainly, LGBT film has spawned a larger festival circuit and more specialty distribution companies than most any other niche of comparable (or even much larger) size.

But this chapter is not meant to be an instruction guide for

LGBT-themed films; rather it is a demonstration of the power and methods of niche distribution and the methods that can be employed to access its lessons. As queer film IS seen as too niche by many, certainly a number of our fair readers will now figure this chapter is not for them, and skip on to the next one. That would be a shame.

Remember, no film lives in a vacuum, and gay viewers may also be Jewish, Latino, women, environmentalists and care about human rights. The best success stories occur when such niches are made to work together, (a fact that can be illustrated time and time again), and where niche distribution techniques can be put to their most powerful use. This work is so important, and yet it is done well by so few that we want to highlight niche-based companies that are working, as we are, in the grassroots arena.

Independent, niche-based marketing and grassroots distribution is now considered a staple of a successful indie release, and as such there are a number of companies that have sprung up to provide these crucial services of grassroots outreach, booking and promotion to the many niches that can be identified for indie film. Some examples include Film Sprout, political activist film pioneer Brave New Films and long-time pioneer Women Make Movies. Of course, we at The Film Collaborative (and our other company, a for-profit called New American Vision) do this work for non-profit organizations, film festivals and sometimes other distributors. These companies seek to turn films into community "calls-to-action," and generate awareness and revenue for films by directly addressing niche communities with a grassroots/community organizing message that can turn the tide for independent films.

Of these companies, one of the best known and most respected "community organizers" in the current marketplace is Caitlyn Boyle's Film Sprout, a highly selective agency which chooses only three films a year for full-scale grassroots booking services. In describing their work, Film Sprout calls itself "a booking agency that broadens the audience and social impact of films through public screening events. Bringing films beyond the traditional cinema and into grassroots institutions, Film Sprout helps filmmakers secure revenue, swell viewership, and spark social change...and all with the potential to attract a high-volume of public screenings hosted by campuses and social action organizations nationwide and to enhance [a film's] public impact by harnessing the enthusiasm and organizing power of grassroots groups." Recent successful films handled by Film Sprout include *Pray the Devil Back To Hell, The Garden, Dirt! The Movie, Race to Nowhere* and *A Small Act* (a Film Collaborative film for film festival distribution).

FOR THE BIBLE TELLS ME SO

For The Bible Tells Me So *directed by Daniel Karslake*

It was 1998, and a young television producer named Daniel Karslake was interning at a PBS TV series called "In the Life," at the time one of the only shows on TV dealing with gay and lesbian issues. To earn a living, Karslake was a fundraiser for New York's famous Riverside Church, a notably "liberal" church in Manhattan. A church-going person himself, Karslake pitched a story to "In The Life" about an out lesbian theologian at Harvard School of Divinity – a subject mixing religion and homosexuality which even "In The Life" found frighteningly controversial; they were, after all, a PBS show dependent on government funding. Despite their reservations PBS gave Karslake the greenlight and the show aired the segment.

The very next day Karslake got the following email from a boy in Iowa.

> *Last week I bought the gun. Yesterday I wrote the note. But last night I happened to turn on your show and just knowing that someday I might be able to go back into my church with my head held high, I threw the gun in the river. My mom never has to know.*

Many hundreds of such emails from LGBT people of faith across the country followed, and it quickly became apparent to Karslake that he had found a calling through film. He quit his day job and became a religion segment producer for "In The Life." In 2002 he saw the Michael Moore documentary *Bowling for Columbine*—one of the first mega-hit, issue-oriented documentaries of recent times – and realized he could expand his focus beyond segment TV to a full-blown documentary. In 2003, openly gay Bishop-elect Gene Robinson became a national story that lit a match at the nexus of religion and sexual orientation, and Karslake had found a documentary subject and a central character that would send him on a four-year odyssey to finish his first film, entitled *For the Bible Tells Me So.*

Here is a synopsis of the film:

> *Can the love between two people ever be an abomination? Is the chasm separating gays and lesbians and Christianity too wide to cross? Is the Bible an excuse to hate?*
>
> *Through the experiences of five very normal, very Christian, very American families—including those of former House Majority Leader Richard Gephardt and Episcopal Bishop Gene Robinson—we discover how insightful people of faith handle the realization of having a gay child. Informed by such respected voices as Bishop Desmond Tutu, Harvard's Peter Gomes, Orthodox Rabbi Steve Greenberg and Reverend Jimmy Creech, For the Bible Tells Me So offers healing, clarity and understanding to anyone caught in the cross-hairs of scripture and sexual identity.*

Of course, no matter how powerful a subject a documentary tackles – and no matter how hungry an audience might be for the message—it is just a tree falling in the forest until it finds a platform to reach its audience. As is so often the case with successful documentaries, *For the Bible* had its first big break when it was accepted into the documentary competition at the 2007 Sundance Film Festival.

Karslake echoed a sentiment expressed by many filmmakers:

> **Daniel Karslake:** *We had some interested parties before, but once we were chosen as one of the 16 competition documentaries at Sundance everything changed. Suddenly every festival and every distributor contacted us and wanted to see the film. There was definitely a "Sundance effect."*

To maximize this "Sundance effect," Karslake signed on high-profile sales agents/film strategists Cinetic Media for the Festival, where the film was sold to Sundance Channel for U.S. TV and most importantly, to First Run Features for all other North American rights.

While the terms of the deal were not disclosed, it is what happened next that makes *For the Bible* such an inspirational story of niche distribution.

At first, both Cinetic and First Run (as well as filmmaker Karslake) were very wary of the gay niche, believing that the film should not be pigeonholed as a gay film for gay audiences, but rather for the uninitiated, largely straight people of faith in the so-called "red states." People who, as Karslake explains, "understood the teachings of Christ, but couldn't square that message with the Church's attitudes towards gay people." As such, the film spent the first few months of its post-Sundance life playing the larger "non-gay" international and doc festivals, winning awards at festivals such as Full Frame and the Audience Award for "Best Documentary" at Seattle International.

For the Bible eschewed the spring LGBT festival circuit, and even chose to skip San Francisco's Frameline—well known as the world's oldest and largest gay and lesbian film festival. For reasons unknown to Karslake, however, First Run Features chose to accept the film's first queer booking at Outfest Los Angeles, a festival held in early summer and which is closely watched by LGBT Industry folks. "I thought gay people would probably hate it," said Karslake, citing general hostility toward religious issues in the Community, supported by his earliest experiences with "In The Life." However, *For the Bible* would go on to win the Audience Award at Outfest, a major validation that would pave the way for launching the film and which would lead to startling results.

Following the cue from earlier awards as well as Outfest, *For the Bible* rocketed through both the summer/early fall international festivals _and_ now also the LGBT circuit, building toward theatrical release in October. Along with the Festival accolades, another key aspect of niche buzz marketing kicked in during this period—namely a tremendous surge in LGBT groups outreaching to their memberships to spread the word about the film.

Most notable was the nationwide support of the gay civil rights organization Human Rights Campaign (HRC), well known as the best-funded, best politically connected of the gay political groups, with nearly a million people on its mailing lists. Prior to Sundance, Karslake had shown a six-minute trailer at HRC's National Convention, and the response and support for the movie was immediate and powerful. Mobilizing both its resources and its chapters, HRC encouraged its members to buy tickets for members for the theatrical opening weekend bookings, just to help make sure the initial release numbers were strong. Also prior to Sundance, Karslake showed the same six minutes at the National Convention of PFLAG (Parents and Friends of Lesbians and Gays), gaining support from its nearly 200,000 membership base.

First Run opened the film in New York City's Quad Theater in early October to a strong result, nearly $10,000 in the first weekend. Capitalizing quickly, First Run moved wider to the Landmark Theatres of Los Angeles, Palm Springs, San Diego, San Francisco, Berkeley, Philly, Boston, Portland, and Minneapolis—all typical big cities on the art-house circuit that include large gay populations. Within a week the film was in St. Louis, Springfield (MO), Austin, Dallas, Atlanta, Salt Lake City, Denver, Santa Fe, Orlando, and New Orleans…and then Charlotte, Tempe, Hartford, Fargo, Tulsa, etc. Choosing both full-week runs and then smaller, limited engagements at regional independent theaters, First Run was able to support the release for nearly six months, finally ending sometime in March 2008 with a gross of around $309,000. Karslake estimates that the film had some sort of theatrical presence in approximately 120 markets, a real eye-opener for a doc distributed by a small indie company.

Shortly into the theatrical run is when the real "miracle" started to happen. In addition to continuing to travel the film both theatrically and along the festival circuit, First Run set up a section of its website to invite community screenings of the film. In early November 2007 the first churches starting calling and booking the film for local, church-based screenings. After churches, it spread to university religion departments, sociology departments, religious conventions, etc. From November 2007 until January 2009—well over a year—scarcely a calendar day went by that the film was not playing in *several cities at once*, often in multiple churches, festivals, and theatrical venues all at the same time. In total, from the time that First Run starting posting the venues on its website soon after Outfest, the film recorded more than *600 engagements* around the country, mostly in small and mid-sized towns, and very often in the heart of the Bible Belt. Rather than just take our word for it, download the PDF (http://www.sellingyourfilm.com/NIC-57.html) for the full story as laid out in a table of bookings.

> **Karslake:** *Just a few years ago, the Bible Belt hadn't yet gotten into the conversation around homosexuality and religion, unlike the discussion that has developed around gay marriage today. Most of the time, maybe 70% of the time, it was small gay groups alerting other small gay groups about the film, and those groups contacting First Run and finding venues in which to show the film to the wider (non-gay) community at large. And then word would catch on, and people would want to be a part of the discussion. Just about everywhere, audience turn-outs were tremendous, and sell-outs were common.*

Karslake, who spent much of the year travelling from screening to screening (constantly amazed himself by the reaction), cites one particular screening in conservative Blacksburg, VA that typified the experience. Still relatively early in the rapid expansion of the

film, a small gay group booked a local theater to show the film…
and warned Karslake before the screening that there probably
wouldn't be more than 25 people in the audience (those were the
kinds of numbers they were used to at their events). Still, they must
have hoped for a better turnout because they booked the 700-seat
Lyric Theater for the event. To everyone's surprise, approximately
1,200 people showed up for the screening, and approximately 500
people had to be turned away.

The effect didn't just stop with live screenings either. Churches eager for the conversation would order DVDs for their whole
congregations. When the 2008 National Convention of the United
Methodist Church met to change their book of common prayer to
stop condemning gay people, they ordered one DVD for each of
their 900 voting members. A similar order was placed on behalf
of 900 Bishops in advance of the 2008 Worldwide Anglican Com-
munion. In each case, Karslake added, his distributor, First Run
Features found a way to make the DVDs available at a cost that
worked for all parties involved.

On the subject of cost (and return), it should be noted that First
Run Features chose not to share all of its numbers and strategies in
this story, instead choosing to say in print:

> **First Run Features:** *First Run Features does not provide
> financial information for public case studies on the films it
> handles. We can tell you this: we booked the film in the-
> aters across the country and worked with the filmmakers
> and related organizations to spread the word. We also had
> excellent publicists working on it. Separately, we created a
> special tour with screenings in churches, community groups
> and non-profit organizations. Approximately half a year
> after the theatrical openings we released the film on DVD.*
>
> *All of the above were very successful (for a serious documen-
> tary), and the film continues to sell very well on home video*

*and rentals to non-profit venues. Meanwhile, after conclud-
ing its first window TV, For the Bible Tells Me So is available
on* Netflix Watch Now *and other Internet platforms.*

*If we told everyone how to do it, then wouldn't everyone just
do it themselves—DIY-style?*

While they are certainly being much more than modest with this last statement (just labor and coordination must have been extraordinary, not to mention the obvious bravery, skill and relationships involved with booking such an extensive theatrical for an issue-oriented doc), there are also pre-existing standards and numbers that we, as the reading public, can apply toward figuring out the kinds of numbers this sort of "non-theatrical explosion" must have generated.

LGBT Festivals are well known to pay rental fees in the range of about $500 for such films, and educational/community-based screenings are understood to run anywhere from $200—$500 for screenings as well. As such, even very quick math has to run the more than 500 festival and community-based screenings listed on the website into the healthy six-figures…a figure which is truly awe-inspiring for a small doc. We can only assume that both First Run and the filmmaker were able to monetize the film to this degree, or indeed even beyond. We may never know for sure (because Karslake needs to honor the terms of his agreement with First Run), but we can easily see that such success is possible. Take note filmmakers: you too can achieve such success.

So, beyond filmmaker and distributor skill, why did it happen and what are the take-aways here? Clearly, *For the Bible Tells Me So* becomes a discussion about the ability to find a niche for such specific content, as well as the timing of the message. Indeed, a niche itself is all about timing, for once a particular niche has had its hunger satiated with content, it may not be as willing to turn out again.

In the case of *For the Bible*, the film found a niche that in many ways cobbled together strange bedfellows around a single issue. Embraced (or at least viewed) by progressive film festival and art-house theatergoers, rural as well as big-city gay activists and religious Christians alike, *For the Bible* becomes a fascinating story of how niche films find their audiences in the fractured contemporary distribution landscape.

UNDERTOW (CONTRACORRIENTE)

Undertow, *directed by Javier Fuentes-León*

Borrowing on the lessons of *For the Bible Tells Me So*, the 2010 Peruvian ghost story and melodrama by Javier Fuentes-León entitled *Undertow* (*Contracorriente* in its native Spanish) was another film to ride major international film festival success to strategic niche distribution in multiple niches…primarily driven by LGBT audiences around the world.

Yet another film to feel the "Sundance effect," *Undertow* was accepted into Sundance 2010 (after its world premiere at San Sebastian in Spain) as a blip on the map…a small, gay-themed movie from Peru by a first-time director who had grown up in Peru but who had moved to LA some 20 years earlier. To be sure, the project had been noted, nurtured and tracked for years by numerous filmmaking labs such as Outfest's Screenwriting Lab, Film Independent, the Berlin Talent Campus, and Curso De Desarrallo de Proyectos Cinematográficos Iberoamericanos (Course of Development of Iberoamerican Film Projects). Javier Fuentes notes about this last lab:

> **Javier Fuentes-León:** *At least that's what it was called back in 2005, when I did it. It takes place in Madrid for a month and a half and they invite 20 projects from Latin America and (I think) 20 projects from Spain. It is sponsored by the Fundación Carolina and the Casa América. My mentors were Lucrecia Martel and Vicente Leñero (screenwriter of* The Crime of Father Amaro *and* Midaq Alley*).*

It was a wonderfully written gay ghost story from Peru that one wasn't likely to see every day…so it garnered significant Industry support, well-wishers and money along its way toward completion, and being included in various screenwriting labs was an encouraging indicator of its potential. Yet it wasn't until it won the 2010 Sundance World Cinema Audience Award that it emerged as the kind of "niche juggernaut" that it would quickly become.

Here is a synopsis of the film:

> *Miguel is a handsome, young and beloved fisherman in Cabo Blanco, a small fishing village on the Northern coast of Peru, where the community has deep-rooted religious traditions. Miguel is married to the beautiful Mariela, who is*

7-months pregnant with their first child, but Miguel harbors a scandalous secret; he is having a love affair with another man, Santiago, a painter who is ostracized by the townsfolk for being both agnostic and open about his sexuality.

When Santiago drowns accidentally in the ocean's strong undertow, he cannot pass peacefully to the other side. He returns after his death to ask Miguel to look for his body and bury it according to the rituals of the town. Miguel must choose between sentencing Santiago to eternal torment or doing right by him and in turn, revealing their relationship to Mariela and the entire village. Miguel is forced to deal with the consequences of his acts and to come to terms with who he really is, even if by doing so he risks losing the people he loves the most.

With sweeping images of the beautiful Peruvian coastline, Undertow (Contracorriente) *is the emotional intersection of contemporary sexuality, confronted by tradition and belief. This sexy and evocative love story is the feature film debut of Javier Fuentes-León and stars Manolo Cardona* (Beverly Hills Chihuahua *and the hugely popular telenovela series,* Sin Tetas No Hay Paraiso. *Cardona was also named by People en Espanol as one of its 50 Most Beautiful People in 2005). The film also stars Cristian Mercado (Che) and Tatiana Astengo. The film was produced by Javier Fuentes-León and Rodrigo Guerrero* (Maria Full of Grace *and* Dog Eat Dog*).*

Sold by Shoreline Entertainment to Wolfe Releasing for North American Rights, and working with The Film Collaborative for both festival and theatrical rights, the film shot out of the gate at Sundance 2010, garnering immediate attention from other film festivals around the globe.

The quickest niche on the uptake for *Undertow* Festival distribution in the U.S. was the Latino Film Festival circuit, as the initial post-Sundance bookings went quickly to the Miami International Film Festival (well known as the most important hub in most Latin media markets in the U.S.), San Diego Latino Film Festival, Cinema Latin American in Montreal, Denver Latino, Chicago Latino, Latin Wave Houston, etc.

Slowly, almost inexorably, the other two niches activated by the buzz of *Undertow*, i.e., those international festivals drawn to the Sundance Audience Award and LGBT film festivals worldwide, began to overtake the Latin niche. By late spring 2010 gay film festivals such as Boston LGBT, Inside Out Toronto, Jacob Burns Film Center, Fairy Tales Calgary, Seoul LGBT, and into Frameline, Outfest, Philly QFest, Newfest NYC, Tokyo International L&G, etc., had begun to dominate. While Latin, Peruvian-specific, and general International film festivals continued to book the film at a healthy rate, the well-established, ever-eager, and well-paying LGBT Film Festival circuit began to dominate the distribution landscape for the film.

Now, more than a year-and-a-half after its world premiere, the film has played at more than 150 film festivals worldwide, a little more than half of which have been queer-specific. The financial upshot of the Festival circuit has been just above $70,000 in Festival booking fees alone.

But it is what *Undertow* did with its Festival fees that makes this story truly unique. A portion of the festival revenue was reinvested into a theatrical release—creating a unique DIY/hybrid release strategy that did not require out-of-pocket expense from the producers, or any daunting investment from a third party. This is a model that we believe is worth exploring for many successful niche films that can earn significant revenue on the Festival circuit.

The theatrical was financed mostly by The Film Collaborative using the festival revenues due to the producers. Wolfe also wanted to get involved so they added in and recouped money too, which otherwise would have been fronted and recouped by TFC. The initial P&A budget was $20,000, but it jumped up to $36,000, in part because of supplementary ads for the Oscar campaign when the film became Peru's official Oscar submission. The budget also went up as the film succeeded and we expanded the release. The film was booked into 21 cities. The box-office gross was $108,620.19 and we recouped the theatrical budget with the film rental, which was usually either 35% or 40% of the gross per market (and Landmark of course has its standard calendar fees). We deliberately had two art campaigns, one general audience oriented (the same poster image that was used at San Sebastian and Sundance and for most of the theatrical releases), and a more gay-male targeted image). We took a 15% Fee off of the film rental (money received from theatres).

To support the theatrical release, a number of basic grassroots/niche outreach tactics were employed. The lowest hanging fruit was all the many film festivals where the film had played, which were each solicited for email blasts/Facebook posts and Tweets announcing the theatrical release to their membership and followers. This included large and active non-gay-specific lists such as the Sundance Film Festival, Latino niche festivals (especially the Chicago Latino Film Festival, which had initially been booked for no festival screening fee with the caveat that they would heavily promote the film upon its release), as well as large gay festivals such as Frameline San Francisco Gay and Lesbian Film Festival, Outfest Los Angeles, and NewFest NY, (all key markets for *Undertow*).

Significant outreach was made to Peruvian community groups, especially in New York and Los Angeles (i.e., Peruvian consulates, Peruvian social clubs, restaurants, meet-up groups etc.). In addition, the large national and local Latino groups based predominantly in Los Angeles were solicited for grassroots marketing support, most notable of which was the National Association of Latino

Independent Producers (NALIP), which blasted often about the film to its heavily sought-after list of Latino film professionals. They helped spread the word further about the film by naming *Undertow* its Estela Award winner for best narrative feature. Examples of other groups contributing to the cause were UCLA's Latin American Institute, the Mexican Consulate of Los Angeles, and the University of Guadalajara Foundation via its close connections with the prestigious Guadalajara Film Festival and their access to Latino filmmakers and professionals based all over the world.

Sheri Candler, (social network marketing strategist and co-author of this book), helped us with social network marketing. She researched all of the blogs and publications that had previously mentioned or reviewed the film to tell them about its release schedule so they could do a follow-up piece encouraging their readers to go and see it if they missed it at festival. She also researched and contacted LGBT organizations and South American organizations in the cities where the film would be playing with language they could include in their blog posts, newsletters and social media pages (mainly links to post for screening information), and suggested that it could be a great night out for their members.

> **Sheri Candler:** *Some came back thanking me for notification and asking where they could buy tickets, what theater exactly, screening times (information clearly written in the original message.) While I could have answered them with just a link to the theater, I generally went out of my way to list the theater, the address, screening times and a link to the box-office or ticket site. When you make things super-easy and convenient for someone, they will take action.*

In return, some posted video of their experience of the film.

> **Sheri:** *I also kept Google Alerts for the film, and whenever someone wrote a review or posted news about the film, I*

On the general publicity side we worked with Kelley Hargraves (general/film press) and Juan Pacheco (Latino press) in Los Angeles and Stephen Raphael & Emma Griffiths (general/film press) and Stacey Rodriguez (Latino press) in New York. Their fees were extremely reasonable and extremely worth it.

TFC's connection to the film started with our having met Javier Fuentes through Outfest, and we helped get his project into the Outfest Screenwriting Lab, which bolstered his connection to Sundance (there are layers of connections between Sundance and Outfest). Later of course, the film was an official Sundance selection in 2010 and went on to win the World Cinema Audience prize.

Internationally, *Undertow* has been sold by Shoreline and/or the film's producers to: USA (Wolfe), Spain (Karma Films), UK/Ireland (Axiom), France (Outplay), Germany (GM Films), Benelux (Cinemien), Dominican Republic/Puerto Rico (Wiesner Distribution), Bolivia, Ecuador (Escalon Films), Brazil (Festival Filmes), Italy (Atlantide), Australia (SBS Television), Taiwan (Joint Entertainment) and Turkey (Digiturk). It is important to note that these distributors represent a mix of companies focused on LGBT cinema (Wolfe, Outplay, GM Films, Atlantide, etc.) – while others are more broadly focused. This of course mirrors *Undertow*'s niche experience overall.

Javier Fuentes speaks to the demographic appeal of the film and the various campaigns in the interview clip.

The film was released theatrically in Peru and Colombia, but the producers did not sell the film to a distribution company. Instead, they hired one in each country to help us with the theatrical release. In Colombia it was CineColombia and in Peru it was New Century Films. In Peru the DVD sales are being handled by Butaca Peru.

The budget of the film was around $900,000. The financing came from 4 different countries and was about half soft money, half private money. The soft money came from: Germany (NRW Filmstiftung), France (Fonds Sud), Peru (Conacine), Colombia (Fondo de Cine Colombiano) and Peru/Colombia (Ibermedia). Private money came from: Colombia (Dynamo Private Film Fund) and Peru (Private investor). The soft money doesn't need to be paid back, but the private money does, (108% of their investment).

Regarding *Undertow*'s DVD and VOD/Digital distribution in the US, the release is brand new and it is too soon to get any numbers, although its DVD/digital distributor, Wolfe Releasing/Wolfe Video notes it was in overages after paying a $100,000 MG two weeks into the release, and in part credits the theatrical for that success. Wolfe added that it exceeded MG by 50% in overages to filmmaker within the first month of release. It should be noted that Wolfe did a five-figure Broadcast deal with HBO Latino.

Some Wolfe Marketing & Advertising highlights (from them):

- Wolfe leverages client relationships with VOD, EST and DVD retailers to further market films. Wolfe also employs print and on-line media to advertise films to niche and trade buyers.

- Gay Pride month features on the home page of iTunes
- Advertising and editorial coverage in Library trade magazines
- Amazon pairings
- E-blasts to over 16,000 DVD retail buyers
- Trailers played via Screenplay in over 1000 video stores
- Posters shipped to over 10,000 retailers for window placement
- Insert cards promoting DVD and VOD in over 100,000 DVD's
- Featured in multiple mailers sent to exclusive Wolfe mailing list of LGBT film buyers
- Heavy placement on WolfeVideo.com and specialty websites
- Social Networking: Wolfe's manages QMovieBlog.com and Wolfe's social network strategy includes a variety of ongoing campaigns across all major platforms. Wolfe has a particularly substantial and active following on Twitter, Facebook and YouTube. Many of Wolfe's most successful YouTube promotions generated over 800,000 hits.

Wolfe's *Undertow* publicity launched over 100 reviews and listings in print, online, on radio and TV; PR also included special outreach to Latino press. In the weeks leading up to the release, Wolfe via publicity firm MPRM secured lots of great reviews and LGBT and Latino press and also 90 regional listings in 25 cities—several multiple times—in Coming to DVD lists. (Cities ranged from Riverside California to Tupelo Mississippi).

DVD & DIGITAL HIGHLIGHTS FROM WOLFE

DVD highlights: *Undertow* was released in June to take advantage of Wolfe's considerable relationships with gay pride programs in traditional retail: Barnes & Noble Store placement on D-Wall and key website exposure, distributor mailers and spiff programs, highlights on Amazon.com, special retailer sales & rebate programs, creation and placement of gay sections in traditional retail such as Best Buy and unique promotions for libraries

Mainstream DVD Retailers included Barnes & Noble, BN.com, FYE stores, Hastings, Fry's, Amoeba, Newbury Comics, Amazon.com, Netflix, Midwest Tape (Library Market), Rentrak, J&R, Borders and ISO Book Club.

Wolfe has long-standing relationships with consumers and specialty retailers; 25% of sales are generated from this unique outreach.

VOD carriage (which in this case it did via Warner Brothers digital): Direct TV, Comcast, Time Warner, Walmart, Best Buy, Cox, Echo Star, Verizon, Charter, AT&T, TVN, iTunes, Amazon and Blockbuster.com, Vudu and Internet promotions with Xfinity.

It should be noted that Wolfe does Netflix directly, and also now has its own YouTube Rental channel (as does TFC).

FURTHER INTO THE LAVENDER NICHE DIVIDE

While films like *For the Bible Tells Me So* and *Undertow* launched at a major "non-gay" festival (Sundance for both) and were also beneficiaries of multiple niches (LGBT and faith-based for the former, gay and Latino for the latter), many other films these days find their audiences almost exclusively within the LGBT community and experience very little crossover. While this is often a source of frustration for many filmmakers, other filmmakers go into the distribution process fully embracing this cultural reality and harvest the landscape of queer distribution to significant success.

Examples of recent films we can examine further in the LGBT niche are: *Were the World Mine* by Tom Gustafson, and Casper Andreas' prolific LGBT output, most specifically two of his more recent films *The Big Gay Musical* and *Violet Tendencies.*

It is worth noting again that not only gay films find singular success within their given niche; we can also find numerous examples within niches like "Latino" (i.e. Lionsgate's *La Mujere de Mi Hermano*), the many Bollywood-focused films of Eros Entertainment, or the Jewish-focused niche films of The National Center for Jewish Film at Brandeis University. In today's marketplace, it is critical for filmmakers to understand the potential niche audience for their films, and to aggressively engage them. But here we focus on "the gay," as a demonstration of the mechanics that drive niche distribution forward.

Originally from Sweden, Casper Andreas studied acting and filmmaking in New York and Los Angeles. His first five features have all opened theatrically in the U.S. and have been released in various markets around the world. His latest film, *Going Down in LA-LA Land* is currently playing festivals.

We selected Casper because he has been consistently DIY focused and he explains why in the interview clip.

This is how Casper promotes his films in every email he sends:

Casper Andreas
Embrem, LLC
www.embrem.com

Now playing festivals:
GOING DOWN IN LA-LA LAND
www.embrem.com/lalaland

Now on VOD & DVD
VIOLET TENDENCIES. Check out the trailer
www.violettendenciesmovie.com

WERE THE WORLD MINE AND THE FILMS OF CASPER ANDREAS

Were the World Mine, *directed by Tom Gustafson*

Gill Holland referred the filmmakers to us before TFC had

launched, and so we worked with them under the banner of our for-profit, New American Vision.

Were the World Mine, a multi-award winning musical romance from 2009 that brought a fresh, gay, charming take to Shakespeare's Midsummer Night's Dream, is described at IMDB as follows:

> *If you had a love-potion, who would you make fall madly in love with you? Timothy, prone to escaping his dismal high school reality through dazzling musical daydreams, gets to answer that question in a very real way. After his eccentric teacher casts him as Puck in A Midsummer Night's Dream, he stumbles upon a recipe hidden within the script to create the play's magical, purple love-pansy. Armed with the pansy, Timothy puckishly imposes a new reality by turning much of his narrow-minded town gay, beginning with the rugby-jock of his dreams. Ensnaring family, friends and enemies in this chaos, Timothy forces them to walk a mile in his musical shoes. Of course, as Shakespeare wrote…"the course of true love never did run smooth," and everyone's in for a bumpy ride.*

Tom Gustafson (Director, Co-Writer, and Producer) and Cory Krueckeberg (Co-Writer/Producer) were interviewed.

CASPER ANDREAS' FILMS AND *WERE THE WORLD MINE*: DIY FESTIVALS AND THEATRICAL DISTRIBUTION

Casper comments on his festival strategy and experience:

> **Casper** *Andreas: My films so far, having mostly been made with a gay audience in mind, have not gotten into any of the top mainstream festivals." When we asked him how much he spends to "open" at the festival and for publicists etc., Casper noted, "I usually spend a few thousand dollars on a website and print material, but I mostly do my own P.R. for festivals. I have hired publicists though, to help me with my*

theatrical and DVD releases.

Violet Tendencies played at festivals in more than 60 cities around the world.

> **Casper:** *I try to play as many festivals as possible, and I always try to get a screening fee. Festivals can be good PR, but I do feel part of what my films bring in from tickets sales should go back to the production company and my investors. If a festival absolutely won't do a screening fee I make sure to get an invitation for me and/or my lead actors. I feel that meeting audiences, discussing the film, and talking about my other films, increases the PR value of playing the festival. I also sometimes arrange to be able to set up a table and sell DVDs after screenings. I turn down festivals all the time though, when they want to play my films and won't give me anything in return. Sure, it's great that more people get a chance to see my film on the big screen, but it could also mean that they don't buy it on DVD or VOD later since they already saw it, so generally I refuse to give it away for nothing.*

Regarding the gross revenue from festivals Casper added:

> **Casper:** *For Violet Tendencies we grossed about $30,000 in festival fees. My other most popular films, A Four Letter Word and The Big Gay Musical grossed about the same."*

Outside of the Festival circuit, did you hold community-based Word-Of-Mouth/buzz screenings? Did you feel they were helpful? Do you have any way to empirically back that up?

> **Casper:** *My films sometimes play at Pride events and gay fundraising events.*

Were the World Mine (WTWM) premiered domestically at the

Florida Film Festival and won the Audience Award. WTWM premiered internationally at the Turin GLBT Film Festival and also won the Audience Award. The filmmakers spent about $5k for FF on publicists and the overall fest launch, but they spent a bit more for our "LGBT" film festival premiere in Miami two months later, where they were booked as the Closing Night film. "That's where we threw our official festival premiere party and helped travel/house the cast and crew. By making it a premiere event with cast and crew, it helped us create a nice buzz about the film and get some additional press."

Director Tom Gustafson had this to say about their festival strategy for *Were the World Mine*:

> **Tom Gustafson:** *Our strategy was to get the most respected festival premiere we could secure and then play every festival that would book us after that. From our perspective, the point of making a film is to show it to people. A small film, like WTWM, might never get to as many theatrical screens as it should, so the festival circuit is a great way to have a "theatrical run." And if you play it the right way, on the festival circuit, a small film like ours can make as much money and play to as many people (if not more) as it would in a traditional theatrical run. WTWM works best with a live audience, and after our first few festivals/awards, we required festivals to pay a substantial screening fee and schedule us in featured slots. By the time we finished with festivals, we'd played about 140, won at least 26 awards, made a decent amount of money, generated a huge amount of publicity and created a large, loyal fan base that went on to buy DVDs, CDs, VOD, Digital Downloads and posters. And contrary to popular belief, our festival screenings didn't seem to diminish our traditional theatrical audiences. For example, we sold out as the Closing Night film at NewFest in NYC and still went on to a five week run at Cinema Village in NYC.*

The filmmakers charged between $100 and $1,000 per screening, depending on the size/scope of the festival. They quoted a standard rate, but were more than willing to negotiate. Sometimes the negotiation involved the festival flying and accommodating the Writer and Director for the festival (Tokyo, Dublin, Turin, and Vancouver): sometimes it involved a promise to distribute flyers and other promotional materials at the screening. Overall, they grossed about $52k in cash and thousands more in travel, perks and advertising of the film. (New American Vision advised them on their festival distribution).

Outside of the Festival circuit, did you hold community-based Word-Of-Mouth/buzz screenings? Did you feel they were helpful? Do you have any way to empirically back that up?

> **Tom Gustafson/Cory Krueckeberg:** *No. The festivals we played created more word-of-mouth/buzz than any screening we could have put together. Of about 140 film festivals, about 75% were LGBT film festivals around the world. WTWM became a much talked about event on each of these city's "gay calendars"—usually as the opening or closing night film of the festival. We could never have created more buzz on our own than that.*

CASPER ANDREAS ON HIS THEATRICAL EXPERIENCES:

> **Casper:** *I opened all my films theatrically. For my first film,* Slutty Summer *I spent months on it and did tons of PR. My second film, A Four Letter Word opened in 15 markets. It was very hard to get audiences to fill the theaters in cities where we were not able to do a lot of PR, so although we made money in NYC, we lost money in a lot of other cities. My last few films opened in just a few markets (three to five).* [Note: Casper also books the theatres <u>himself</u>.]

How much did you spend on the theatrical?

Casper: *Generally I spend $1,000-$2,000 on posters, post-cards, and flyers. I spend a few thousand dollars in NYC for sure on ads and marketing; less in smaller cities. When we opened A Four Letter Word in 2008 at the Landmark Theaters I spent maybe $3,000 to get the film onto their digital system. Then I had to make 35 mm trailers, which costs several thousands as well. I haven't done that since. Since I do most of my PR myself with interns (sending out screeners to reviewers, placing ads, setting up interviews, distributing postcards), my PR costs are minimal, though the time commitment is huge.*

How long was the theatrical run?

Casper: *A Four Letter Word played for three weeks in NYC on a full screen. A couple of my other films played for two weeks. In other cities they generally played for just one week.*

How many cities were full-week runs?

Casper: *For my latest theatrical, Violet Tendencies, we had a full-week run only in NYC and LA.*

How many cities were one-night events in traditional theatrical venues?

Casper: *For Violet Tendencies I did a couple of those.*

How much did you GROSS and NET? Can you give a specific on your highest grossing week-long run and lowest grossing week-long run? What about for one-night events?

> **Casper:** *My highest grossing week was the opening week of A Four Letter Word at the Chelsea Clearview in NYC: $15,831. Even though the theater took about two thirds of that we did end up making money in NYC during our three week run. The lowest grossing week was probably a few hundred for the week in Palm Dessert, CA for the same film.*

WERE THE WORLD MINE'S TAKE ON THEIR THEATRICAL:

The filmmakers did do a conventional theatrical release (and our previous company did most of the booking, although we did it for free). "The amount of time spent setting it up is hard to say, as it was spread out over a couple of months. It was a full time job for several weeks leading up to the first release date. Our total spend on the theatrical was about $60k for materials, marketing, ad buys, publicist and deliverables. However, our theatrical run would have been relatively inexpensive had we not had to pay for some of the required print advertisements. For example, our NYC exhibitor required an ad in the NY Times, which cost about $11,000. Ironically, in that same print issue, our review appeared (as a Critics' Pick—complete with a photo) and took up four times as much space as our tiny $11k ad. But I guess we'll never know. Maybe having both the ad and the review solidified our title in people's heads and generated future ticket, DVD, CD, VOD and Digital Download sales. Our sales agent, New American Vision, brokered the deal with Landmark and various other exhibitors, including LA and NYC. We also worked with Emerging Pictures for a few cities (Orly notes: which we connected them to). For additional cities, we booked them ourselves by directly contacting venues that hosted prior successful festival screenings."

How do Niche Films find their Audiences? **209**

How long was the theatrical run?

> Tom/Cory: *It varied by city. NYC was five weeks, SF and Chicago were both two weeks. In all we played about 30 cities in a "conventional theatrical" setting for an overall total of about 40 weeks. (All of those cities were full-week runs).*
>
> *We grossed a total of about $130K over our 30-city run. Our net was about $35K after fees, exhibitor share, etc. Our first weekend at Cinema Village in NYC we had the fourth highest per-screen average in the country. We sold out the entire weekend and for many of the screenings in the following weeks. NYC was our highest grossing city. We spent $60K on the commercial theatrical run, took in about $60K from the festival theatrical run and $35K from the commercial theatrical run. So our net—for what we consider our full "theatrical" run—was an extremely modest $35K.*

WERE THE WORLD MINE'S ADDITIONAL ALTERNATIVE/ HYBRID THEATRICAL:

Aside from the 140 city festival run and 30 city theatrical run, there were a handful of "alternative theatrical" screenings by community groups and universities. The filmmakers spent nothing to book the alternative theatrical release.

> Tom/Cory: *Our approach to all screening—from huge film festivals to tiny campus groups—was to make the film accessible. Some groups have large budgets and some have none. We always quoted our festival rate and then negotiated, (down to zero in some cases). It's a balancing act between give and take. Sometimes by giving everything for nothing you get a lot in return.*

They grossed about $8,000 on their alternative theatrical release.

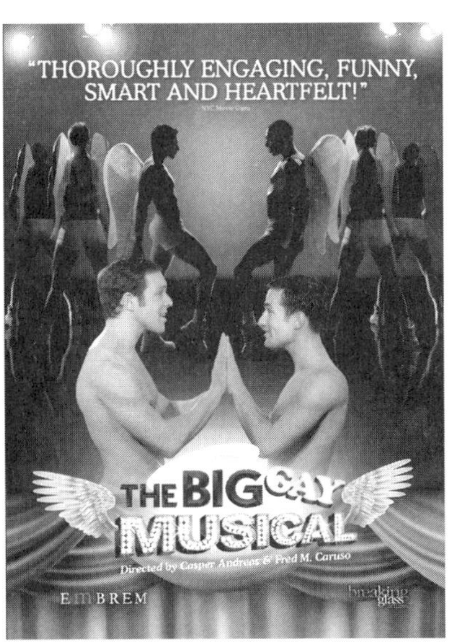

Big Gay Musical, *directed by Casper Andreas & Fred M. Caruso*

CASPER ANDREAS AND *WERE THE WORLD MINE* ON PUBLICITY, GRASSROOTS AND SOCIAL NETWORK MARKETING

How much did you spend for the marketing and promotion of your release?

Casper: [Casper was not completely sure of exact numbers but he noted this:] *It's all tied together with spending money on a theatrical release. I'm hoping I don't have to spend as much money on the DVD/VOD release. I do some campaigns on Facebook and Google from time to time. I'm not spending tens of thousands though, just a few thousand here and there. I know some people say you should, but it's so hard to justify. Will I really get that back in more sales if I do? I don't know. I hire a publicist from time to time to help with doing PR for a theatrical opening or a DVD release, but not every time. Our agreements are confidential and I'd* *rather not discuss them. I spent a lot of money on print ads when I opened* A Four Letter Word *theatrically and I think it was wasted money. For my last films I mostly did targeted advertising online. When I did print ads it was easily $1,000 a week, and I don't think it helped at all. I spend about half that on targeted Facebook ads for some cities, but I'm not sure that's working either. Mostly I focused on getting interviews, articles, and reviews.*

Did you purchase Facebook Ads or Google Ads? How much did you spend? Were they effective?

Casper: *I've tried both. I did some targeted campaigns on Facebook that did increase DVD sales, but it's hard to say how effective they were. I did a few campaigns from time to time on Facebook when* The Big Gay Musical *came out on DVD, spending about $50 per day for a week or two. I linked to my own website, embrem.com, and saw increased sales in 1-2 DVDs, which is less than I spent in income per day. However, I'm hoping that some consumers saw the ad and decided they rather buy from Amazon, or some place where they already have an account set up, since it's more convenient for them.*

Do you have any YouTube stats? Please explain and go into detail if so. What activity led to more views?

Casper: *I've not kept track of activities and what works. Usually, when the trailers are first put on there we try to get them re-posted on blogs, Facebook pages, etc. That usually brings up the numbers a lot at first.*

Did you push any other form of content on the web, e.g., video content? How did you do this? Did you pay for this? Did it help your statistics—#s or $s?

> **Casper:** *I posted behind the scenes videos, etc. It is hard to say if it really matters in terms of sales.*

WERE THE WORLD MINE ON ITS MARKETING

> **Tom:** *From festivals through theatrical, we spent a total of about $25k for all publicity and promotion, personnel, materials and travel, including targeted hand-flyering in NYC during our theatrical run. This spend was part of the previously described $60k spend for distribution—not in addition to. David Magdael & Associates handled all WTWM publicity, from festivals to theatrical. Nevette Previd handled promotion and marketing (including some social media work – not as prevalent in 2008 as it is now), for our theatrical run. Everyone really believed in WTWM and worked hard to bring a tiny film as much attention as they could."*

Did you track your online analytics related to specific promotional activities?

> **Tom/Cory:** *No.*

Did you purchase any media (print ads, radio or TV, web banner ads)? How much did you spend on each?

> **Tom/Cory:** *We purchased print ads in various cities during our theatrical run, spending a total of $19k. Some were required by the exhibitors.*

Did you purchase Facebook Ads or Google Ads?

Tom/Cory: *No.*

Do you have any YouTube stats? Please explain and go into detail if so. What activity led to more views?

Tom/Cory: *It's impossible to really answer this. Our official trailer, which we uploaded to YouTube has around 275K views. Another trailer that a fan made has had the same number of views. Our 'sneak peek' that we put up before the official trailer has 100k views, as does the trailer uploaded by our DVD distributor. In all, there are hundreds of videos on YouTube—mostly made by fans—of or about WTWM.*

The *Were the World Mine* filmmakers did not do any online competitions, push any other form of content or do any other promotions on the web.

THE FILMMAKERS ON ORGANIZATIONAL OUTREACH

When it came to organizational outreach, neither Casper Andreas nor the filmmakers of *Were the World Mine* had any great success.

Tom/Cory: *At first we did some very basic grassroots work ourselves via Facebook and MySpace, but after our first couple of festival successes, the festivals, especially the LGBT festivals, became the primary promotional tool. The LGBT festivals employ a lot of "grassroots organizations" in their usual promotion. In fact, a lot of those festivals are "grassroots organizations" themselves. As for other more high profile 'grassroots organizations,' we did attempt to align with a few (which will remain nameless) in the beginning, some even before we shot the film, but none were interested in getting involved until the film was already a success. Then they started contacting us to try to piggyback on our success after the fact. We did take some minor promotional help from several groups during the theatrical run.*

Unfortunately, we at TFC have experienced the same phenomenon, wherein significant grassroots/organizational involvement is only achievable for a film that is already a success. Grassroots promotion, to be effective, needs to be a win-win for both the film and the organization, so in fact, most organizations only want to spend the time to help a film that they know will bring great attention to them as well. As such, films that have already gained a great deal of traditional "buzz" through Festival play and major press are the ones that organizations will most readily line up to support. This is a difficult "chicken-and-egg-situation" for films looking to generate organizational outreach in the earliest stages of the campaign.

TV, DVD, VOD & DIGITAL, MERCH, DEALS, STRATEGY, PLATFORMS AND REVENUE

About Traditional DVD

How many DVD units did you sell via a distributor?

Casper: *Well it's very hard to answer. I've never sold more than 10,000 DVDs since I started manufacturing them myself. Perhaps Slutty Summer sold more, but I would have to find statements for the last six years and add them all up.*

How much did you receive from the DVD distributor? Are you still owed money?

Casper: *I got an advance of $30,000 for my first film, Slutty Summer. For my second film I got advance offers of close to*

$100,000, but I didn't take them (that included all rights TV/VOD as well). It has only been downhill from there. For The Big Gay Musical I looked into selling off just the DVD rights, and the best offer I got was a $10,000 advance with a 50/50 split from one company. I declined. It seems as if distributors are notoriously late with backend payment. I don't have any horror stories to share though…yet.

How many DVD units did you sell yourself?

Casper: *It's scary how much DVD sales have declined in just a few years. I manufacture my own DVDs now, and so far I might have manufactured 10,000 copies of my top-selling films for the US and Canada. Not a lot.*

How much did you gross?

Casper: *Generally $7-$10 per DVD sold comes back to the production company. 70K-100K actually, if I indeed sold 10K DVDs, but I have not made that much yet on a DVD. Maybe we got back close to 70K on TBGM, but again, that is before my expenses of making the DVDs, shipping, doing my own PR, etc.*

What are your terms with the distributor?

Casper: *I have different terms for different films, and I don't think I'm allowed to discuss them. However, after selling my first film, Slutty Summer to TLA releasing, and seeing how much they made on it (I only got a small percentage, less than 1/4), I never did a regular DVD distribution deal again for the US and Canada. Instead, I manufacture my own DVDs and make a deal with a distributor to do my sales. I did this with TLA for A Four Letter Word and Between Love & Goodbye, and with Breaking Glass Pictures for The Big*

Gay Musical and Violet Tendencies. Since they only make a small percentage on any sales, I find they won't promote these titles as much as they would the ones they make more money on, so I think I could have sold more DVDs (but probably still made less money) on a regular deal. It's hard to know what is best, though. Since few distributors are willing to pick up the DVD rights without VOD and TV, I feel they are pushing me toward self-distribution, as it makes no sense to me to have another middleman for TV and VOD deals. For my new film, Going Down in LA-LA Land I'm considering doing the DVD sales all by myself (unless I get some amazing advance that I can't refuse).

Violet Tendencies *directed by Casper Andreas*

If you buy your DVDs from your distributor—how much do you pay per unit?

> **Casper:** *For me this only applies to my first film,* Slutty Summer. *It started at $10/unit. I think we are down to $5/ unit.*

What has been your overall experience with your DVD distributor?

> **Casper:** *I generally like the people working at the two companies I've been dealing with. Both of them send me very detailed statements, so I'm very happy with that. I like to see where the DVDs have been sold and for how much. TLA has been late with payments, but I'm hoping that will change with the restructuring they are doing. Breaking Glass have generally paid on time so far.*

Were the World Mine did its DVD distribution via Wolfe (and we brokered the deal at the time). It should be noted that we took 15% of MGs only, not backend, and also did the theatrical consultation and booking for free. Deals were always between distributor and filmmaker, as was our style even then.

Wolfe sold approximately 30,000 units for a total of $278,000 in receipts so far, and it sold the film into these retailers:

Amazon.com
Amoeba
Barnes & Noble
Bookspan
BN.com
Borders
Fry's
Hastings
Hollywood Video (R.I.P)
    (where they had the an store promo with trailer playing)
ISO Book Club

J&R
Midwest Tape (Library Market)
Movie Gallery
Newbury Comics
Netflix
Rentrak
TLA
Trans World (FYE stores)

Wolfe's Highlights for *Were the World Mine*

It immediately exceeded $90K MG in overages to filmmaker and went into overages prior to broadcast & VOD sales. It nearly doubled MG in the second year of release;

DVD & VOD/Digital marketing highlights:

- Created LGBT Sections in Best Buy stores nation-wide
- Featured wall placement in June for Gay Pride Month in multiple retailers nationwide
- Created LGBT boutique BarnesandNoble.com
- Featured on Tower.com
- Created call out box on LGBT page on Amazon.com including exclusive clips
- iTunes home page placement
- Included in mailer to library markets, DVD Release Report
- Submitted and then nominated for Amazon.com Windowshop
- Created 2 DVD box covers for different audience appeal
- Marketing promotions included extensive print advertising in conjunction with a contest promotion and cruise line sponsorship
- VOD/Digital carriage: Amazon, Blockbuster.com, iTunes, Cinema Now (Best Buy), VEOH, MySpace, Blockbuster, Direct TV, Comcast, Time Warner, Cox, Echo Star, Verizon, Charter, AT&T, TVN, Netflix

- The film continues to sell in year 3 on DVD.

Wolfe's direct-to-consumer reach:

- Physical mailing list is 185,000
- E-Wolfetracks (e-newsletter) in 45,000
- QMovieBlog is 48,000

DVD and Other Merchandise Sales from Websites or at Events

What fulfillment company do you use or do you self fulfill?

Casper: *I fulfill my website orders myself.*

How much have you made from your own DVD sales?

Casper: *Between my different films I grossed a few thousand dollars selling off my website and at screenings. (I don't have an exact number available.)*

How much have you made from other merchandise?

Casper: *Very little, although I haven't tried it much. I probably made a few hundred dollars on Slutty Summer T-shirts. I made very little on posters. The Between Love & Goodbye Soundtrack CD has probably grossed $3,000-4,000 (including digital sales).*

Were the World Mine's Soundtrack:

Tom: *We had a couple of offers for a soundtrack distribution deal. One with a major soundtrack label and one from PS Classics, a label that specializes in Broadway cast recording albums and solo albums by Broadway stars. We went* *with PS Classics because we knew that their primary audience would be a large part of our target audience. PS Classics got us physically into all of the major music stores of the time and placed us on iTunes, Amazon…You can find our soundtrack every place where music is sold. They've been great. We benefitted—and still do—from the personal attention from a label that was small enough to really care about our film but prominent enough to release us on every music selling platform available. Our deal with them has actually made us a little money—something we would never have seen from the major labels. And PS Classics also got press for the soundtrack in Playbill!*

Broadcast & VOD/Digital Distribution

Casper's first film was sold to Here TV. He sold three films, *A Four Letter Word*, *Between Love & Goodbye* and *Violet Tendencies* to Logo (part of MTV Networks).

Casper had this to say about the value of the deals:

> **Casper:** *I'm not allowed to say, but I can tell you the deals are structured for 4-5 years. They pay a flat rate in advance and they can then air them as many times and as often as they want. [We know that Logo pays low, medium and high five-figure and occasionally six-figure fees. For example, Were the World Mine and Violet Tendencies both sold for very solid fees to Logo.]*

Casper negotiated the Logo deals himself.

> **Casper:** *Speaking to other filmmakers I knew what to expect, so I didn't see a need to hire a sales agent.*

The Filmmakers on VOD

> **Casper:** *My distributor for Slutty Summer (TLA) hasn't*

Gravitas Ventures licensed *The Big Gay Musical* after reading many positive reviews from its film festival screenings, and worked with Warner Bros. Digital Distribution on the marketing and distribution. *The Big Gay Musical* was distributed in April 2010 to more than 100 cable, satellite, and telco operators, including all major operators like Comcast, Time Warner Cable, Cox, Charter, Cablevision, Verizon and AT&T. The combined cable and digital VOD release means the film was available in over 100 million North American homes. Many operators carried the film for six months.

Casper went back to Gravitas for his next film, *Violet Tendencies,* but that release is too new to discuss in terms of performance and numbers.

Here is something all filmmakers always want to know: How much money have you made from VOD?

Casper: *I didn't get any numbers from Violet Tendencies yet, but for The Big Gay Musical I got around $50,000-$60,000 after a year in release. This includes Internet streaming and downloads.*

Gravitas backed this up stating: "Combining cable VOD, digital and its first Netflix license, the filmmaker will receive royalties in the high five-figures within 18 months of the title's VOD debut."

Wolfe via Warner Brothers got *Were the World Mine* VOD carriage on Direct TV, Comcast, Time Warner Cox, Echo Star, Verizon, Charter, AT&T, TVN, iTunes, Amazon and Blockbuster.com.

The Big Gay Musical was distributed in April 2010 to major digital platforms, including Apple iTunes, Amazon Instant Video, Blockbuster.com, CinemaNow, Netflix SVOD, Sony PlayStation, Microsoft Zune and Vudu.

Gravitas Ventures collaborated with Warner Bros. Digital Distribution on the marketing and distribution. The film will play on each platform for years, and Gravitas and Warner will continue to "merchandize" the content on each storefront. Merchandizing could be adding *The Big Gay Musical* to certain promotional areas (LGBT collection on Apple iTunes), or engaging in new pricing strategies to generate new interest in the title.

Wolfe through Warner Brothers got *Were the World Mine* onto these digital platforms: Amazon, Blockbuster.com, Best Buy, iTunes, and Walmart's. VOD revenue to Wolfe has exceeded $85K (this includes a 5-figure Netflix fee). Wolfe did its digital distribution through Warner Brothers in this case as well.

None of the filmmakers had Apps, but Casper and TFC have been discussing creating one for his works and possibly aggregating others.

On the merch front, none of the filmmakers had any except for Casper for one film.

We were asked not to disclose fees for digital or DVD distribution by in large. In our letter to filmmakers we note what the standard DVD fees are and what is acceptable. On the digital side 15% is a fair fee and 20% and 25% and 30% is not always bad either (though of course we prefer lower), depending on the service. Above that, for a distributor, we generally find unacceptable and most especially if one is not direct but either way.

The LGBT Movie Collection in the iTunes Store. Gravitas and Wolfe both went through Warner Brothers to get The Big Gay Musical *and* Undertow, *respectively, onto iTunes.*

FOREIGN SALES

Casper does his own sales and TFC helped the *Were the World Mine* filmmakers do foreign sales (in the same way we do now, which is by not taking rights and having deals be between the buyer and the filmmaker).

Casper sold off different territories: UK/Ireland, Germany and German-speaking Europe, France and French-speaking Europe, Australia and New Zealand. In one case Taiwan and in one case

Mexico. For a small upfront payment they get all the rights in the territory for 6-10 years. The range for such sales can be as low as just a few thousand to $15,000, and sometimes $20,000, but is usually not any higher than that for an LGBT film with a no-name cast.

Neither of the filmmakers sold just to TV internationally. The deals were all rights deals, and sometimes there are overages and sometimes there are none.

> **Casper:** *I've yet to see any real money on the backend, and with the small advances I'm struggling with trying to figure out if there is a better way to go. Self –distribute a DVD in all of EU somehow? Do my own VOD sales all over the world? Something has to change as I make very little on these international deals.*

When we (TFC) do international sales we often carve out some digital and at least DIY so that filmmakers can still monetize their films directly to fans on platforms that the distributors are not working with, or at least off the filmmakers' own site and Facebook pages, etc. We also advised Casper to do an iPhone App because he's so prolific and has his own brand.

Overall, these filmmakers have the commonality of knowing their audience and knowing how to access it (and the distribution partners do too). These techniques can be applied to knowable niches and provide great guidance for future filmmakers looking to reach their audiences.

Using Peer to Peer (P2P) Methods to Distribute Film?

By Sheri Candler

THE PIRACY PROBLEM

One of the most talked about fears in the film industry today is digital piracy. The digital technology that enables content to reach a worldwide audience at a low price has also enabled a disruption to traditional business models sending industry executives, labor unions, and content owners screaming, "We must do something to control this." At no other time in history has it been possible to make an exact clone of artistic material and circulate it for free, circumventing decades-old copyright protections and the possibility of revenue collection from those copies.

According to the US Government Accountability Report (April 2010), it is nearly impossible to accurately report how much revenue and how many job losses have occurred due to the effects of piracy. There is no government agency that systematically collects or tracks data on the extent of digital copyright piracy[1], and there is no verifiable data that can be relied upon because methodolo-

---

1   "Intellectual Property—Observations on Efforts to Quantify the Economic Effects of Counterfeit and Pirated Goods," *United States Government Accountability Office, Report to Congressional Committees*, p. 15-16.

gies used are predominantly based on assumptions, often the result of industry speculation with no original data collection being performed. Even the MPAA has had to recant its estimations when it originally reported that 44% of US film industry revenues were being lost to digital file sharing at universities. It scaled back its estimates to 15%.[2] Yet, it is widely regarded within the industry that digital piracy is reducing incentive to produce quality content, costs billions in revenue and accounts for thousands of job losses each year. These are the statistics most referenced to ensure a sense of urgency to enact new legislation.

Efforts at curbing consumer appetite for pirated content have largely relied on the threat of incarceration and/or financial punishment, embarrassment, aggrievement on the part of creators and fears of terrorist/organized crime funding as deterrents. To the average file sharer, often young people with little to lose financially and a shortsighted sense of the future, these methods have proven ineffective. There have been moves in the US to crack down on digital piracy; the most recent is the Protect IP Act (United States Senate Bill S.968), which has been widely backed by artists' rights groups, entertainment labor unions, studios and publishing corporations. The bill proposes to block access to "rogue" or "pirate" websites predominantly outside of the United States that are allegedly dedicated to copyright infringement. The Bill allows the US Justice Department to seek court orders against such sites and seize their information location tools in an effort to render the sites invisible to search engines and to break their Domain Name System ties to web indexes worldwide, thus blocking access.[3] This point is particularly troubling as it means the US would have the

---

2   Justin Pope, "MPAA admits mistake on downloading study," *Newsweek*, Jan 23, 2008. (http://www.sellingyourfilm.com/P2P-74.html)

3   "Protect IP Act," *Wikipedia*. (http://www.sellingyourfilm.com/P2P-76.html)

power to alter the entire Domain Name System registry which powers search of the internet and is a system which is meant to be universal. It is not hard to imagine the corruption that could ensue by allowing a government entity to "filter" any site it finds not in the public interest. DNS manipulation is already used in repressive governments around the world such as some Middle Eastern countries and communist China. Is the US looking to follow in their footsteps all in the name of protecting intellectual property rights especially for large media corporations?

A recent letter to Congress penned by over 90 law professors claims that the Bill is unconstitutional and dangerous to the health of the whole system of the internet because at present "all domain name servers, wherever they may be located on the network, will return the same answer when queried with respect to the internet address of any specific domain name—on which countless numbers of internet applications, at present, are based."[4] Allowing for alteration destroys the whole purpose of having a DNS.

Protect IP Bill also allows for IP owners and the government to seek injunctions against third parties providing services to allegedly infringing sites such as credit card companies and advertising networks, but also any site that provides for posting URL links that could point to infringing sites such as Facebook, Twitter or a blog.[5]

The Bill has received criticism for (1) not being specific enough in what constitutes an infringing website; (2) raises free speech concerns by allowing sites to be filtered even if parts of the site contain legal content or non infringing sites being filtered that are interdependent through the use of virtual hosting or sub domain

---

4   Emma Woollacott, "Protect IP Act more restrictive than Chinese law, say profs," *TGDaily.com*, July 7, 2011. (http://www.sellingyourfilm.com/P2P-77.html)

5   Abigail Phillips, "The 'Protect IP' Act: COICA Redux," *Electronic Frontier Foundation*, May 12, 2011. (http://www.sellingyourfilm.com/P2P-78.html)

hosting[6]; and (3) its mandated DNS filtering will threaten the System's ability to provide universal naming, a primary source of the internet's value as a single, unified, global communications network.[7]

Opponents of the Bill include Google, Yahoo, Electronic Frontier Front and American Express. Even the LA Times newspaper, usually a staunch follower of anything the Hollywood industry supports, has voiced its concerns over the broad definitions of the Bill, particularly in relation to cutting off traffic to offending websites. Companies that operate Domain Name Servers would be required to redirect all traffic away from such websites, but often many websites share or are interdependent on domain names and could be harmed even when they are not infringing. Also, it has been mentioned that simply preventing a domain name from being found in the search registry will do little to curb traffic to the offending website. All that would be needed is a free plug-in that substitutes numeric IP addresses for domain names and the sites will be found in search. The Bill is supported by The National Cable and Telecommunications Association, Microsoft, IATSE, and The Motion Picture Association of America, to name a few.

Similar government measures have been enacted in the UK, France and New Zealand, with Canada and Australia proposing legislation. Spain's proposed law was killed on the eve of its passing when secret cables from the US government were made public on the infamous Wikileaks site and reported to the Spanish public by El Pais. The cables showed threats from the US government to keep Spain on the Special 301 Report, a list of countries that are

---

6   "Protect IP Act Raises First Amendment Concerns," *Blog of the National Coalition Against Censorship*, June 7, 2011. (http://www.sellingyourfilm. com/P2P-79.html)

7   David Kravets, "Internet Researchers Decry DNS-Filtering Legislation," *Wired*, May 31, 2011 (http://www.sellingyourfilm.com/P2P-80.html)

considered a threat to US intellectual property interests. Inclusion on the Watch List can place extreme political pressure on government officials and can lead to trade sanctions for the countries listed if they do not change their laws to mirror US guidelines.[8]

THEY'RE STEALING MY WORK

Supporters of the current proposed legislation and many artists themselves view online dissemination and enjoyment of their work without permission or payment as theft. The correct term is copyright infringement, as the accused "thief" does not actually deprive the owner of their property in the way that stealing a possession such as a car or a pair of jeans would. Copyright infringement is the unauthorized or prohibited use of works under copyright protection infringing the copyright holder's exclusive rights, such as the right to reproduce or perform, or to make derivative works.[9] Many rights holders object to this explanation because they see the harm from physical theft (deprivation from use of an object) and copying (financial deprivation) as the same thing. Those in favor of strong copyright protections also point out that loss of income affects not only the copyright owner, but the workers who reproduce the goods and sell them in the marketplace. Without the business model protected by intellectual property rights, there would be no incentive to create and innovate.

The Obama administration sees digital piracy as a threat to US economic strength and has vowed to fight to preserve the livelihood of US artists and companies that are now threatened because their business models all rely heavily on selling copies of work.

---

8   Gwen Hinze, "Not-So-Gentle Persuasion: US Bullies Spain into Proposed Website Blocking Law," *Electronic Frontier Foundation*, December 17, 2010. (http://www.sellingyourfilm.com/P2P-81.html)

9   "Copyright Infringement," *Wikipedia*. (http://www.sellingyourfilm.com/P2P-82.html)

BUT WHAT IF YOU GAVE YOUR WORK AWAY?

Non-supporters of strong copyright, or indeed any copyright, point out that inventors and creatives rarely start their process motivated by making money. It is a great by-product that adds to their ability to create, but would innovation truly cease if creators could not make money? Is monetary value the sole reason for propagation of ideas and innovations? In other words, do artists create only because there is money in it for them? From what I see around me, that can't be the case. There are many more artists in the world creating without financial gain than there are with it.

HOW WOULD THIS WORK?

There is no question that there is consumer demand for entertainment. Content continues to be produced and consumed at ever growing levels. A report just issued by accounting firm PwC predicts that the film industry will continue to grow through 2015 buoyed by the increase in electronic delivery of content. The issue is how to effectively and profitably service the demand. Reliance on control over consumers, high pricing models and artificial scarcity are quickly being undermined by conveniently available content and ever-lowering prices. Emphasis has been placed on stopping file sharing sites rather than figuring out ways to use them advantageously. Wouldn't it be better to think about how this innovation can help accomplish something better, more efficiently and more cost effectively?

There are a few artists experimenting with the new, free distribution methods that the internet affords while building a direct relationship with audiences and making money. Their business models use a combination of keeping production costs low, funding production through donations and grants to mitigate the need to find and repay investors, thinking about alternative revenue streams rather than a reliance on selling copies. This enables them to create an identifiable brand, be innovative in their work and maintain their vision while building a sustainable audience to last throughout their careers. For some, it has also led to financial rewards.

OBSCURITY IS WORSE THAN PIRACY: THE CASE STUDY OF *PIONEER ONE*

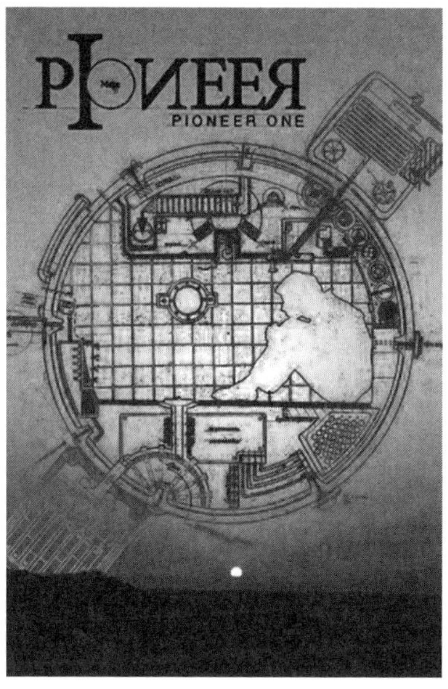

Pioneer One, *an episodic drama series produced by*
Josh Bernhard and Bracey Smith

Pioneer One is an episodic drama series produced by Josh Bernhard and Bracey Smith. The series is notable both for being funded purely through donations and for being the first series created for and released on file sharing networks via VODO.[10] Funding for

____

10 "PioneerOne," *Wikipedia.* (http://www.sellingyourfilm.com/P2P-07.html)

the pilot episode was raised through Kickstarter, and the series has been released using Creative Common License CC BY-NC-SA 3.0.

From the start, *Pioneer One* was intended to be distributed via file sharing, but it was not the team's first experience using that method. Josh Bernhard's debut feature, a micro-budget drama called *The Lionshare*, released in 2009, examined the topic of file sharing and the communities that engage in the activity. The film was shot for $6,000, and Josh knew that it did not have mainstream appeal and was not a candidate for a traditional distribution deal. His real aim behind the project was to make a name for himself and have the film seen by as many people as possible; a goal much like that of many first-time directors.

Josh saw the opportunity to use file sharing sites as a way to reach a mass audience without the need for a distributor or a large budget.

> **Josh Bernhard:** *There is a perception that the only people looking for content on the internet are pirates; that they only want things for free and they are looking to get away with something. That's an artifact of the thinking of people who are in traditional media who are used to doing things a certain way. They can't see file sharing sites as something to take advantage of, only as something to be resisted. For us, the idea was to participate in this new way of disseminating content because we have nothing to lose and everything to gain. As outsiders in the media establishment we needed a way to get our work out there so there was no reason not to embrace it. With* The Lionshare, *I had the idea for a film that I wanted to make and the means to do it and I just wanted it to be seen by as many people as I could.*

Sofie Larson (Alexandra Blatt) on the left and Bracey Smith
discussing a scene in episode 05

The film played the festival circuit for a short time and Josh uploaded it to many P2P sites. That is where the team at VODO saw it and approached Josh to ask if they could host the film on their site.

> **Josh:** *After releasing The Lionshare on VODO, the response was larger than anything I had ever seen previously* [at this writing, it has been downloaded over a half million times]. *I got excited about creating an original series to put out on VODO. Their site was really just starting up and I thought it would be a great thing for them and for us because there would be known content on the site that people would return to over and over, instead of just once in a while, to see what new narrative or documentary films were available. So far, it has been their biggest content success.*

In order to raise money for the pilot episode, Josh and Bracey turned to popular crowd-funding site Kickstarter to collect donations in March 2010. Their goal amount was $6000 and they ended up raising $7485 from 122 backers, mostly in the $10-$50 range.

Using P2P (Peer to Peer) Methods to Distribute Film? **235**

It helped that they had an initial base of supporters from The Lionshare who contributed almost $2000 to the recoupment of the film's production costs through donation. They also solicited blogger attention and posted on popular P2P forums to attract contributions.

> **Bracey Smith:** *I think it had to do with the novelty of the idea and the exposure it was getting. It helped that we had the connections from The Lionshare and using BitTorrent and Pirate Bay as well as getting blogs to cover it.*

The series continues to attract media attention and donations through VODO instead of Kickstarter.

> **Bracey:** *After the pilot went up, people could see what we were doing with the show and how the next step would go, but only if they were a part of it, a part of creating the next episodes. I think that is really an essential part of the crowdfunding effort so far. People felt they were helping to create something, not just giving money to a company to create.*

The series pilot went into production in April 2010 and hit the web on June 16, 2010. To date, the pilot episode has been downloaded over 300,000 times. There are now 4 episodes in release with 2 more planned and over $70,000 raised in all. Reviews from the sci-fi fan community have been strong, with many eager to champion Josh and Bracey for being in charge of creating and distributing their own work.

In total, the series has been downloaded more than 3 million times (it is impossible to track the exact amount). The pilot episode was uploaded on YouTube many times by fans (and they are legally able to do this), the most notable by an account called Tavin15 garnering over 75,000 views.

L-R Eric McClellan (Einar Gunn) and David Collins (John Isgro)

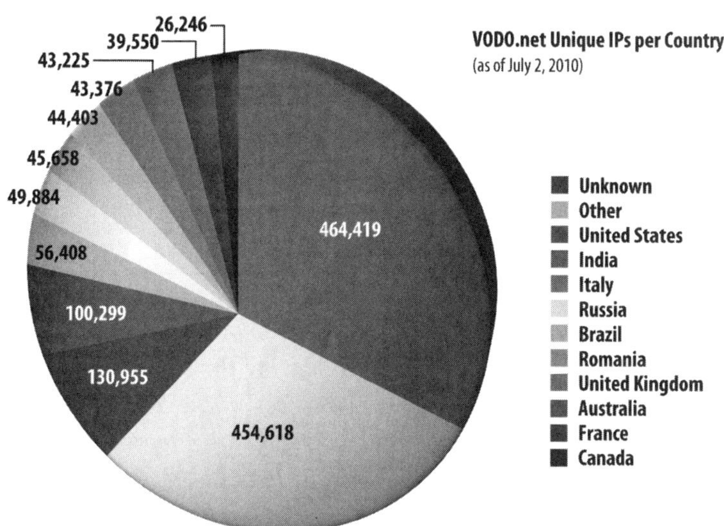

This charter reflects the download activity after the release of the first 2 episodes on VODO.net. Efforts to get deeper analytical data for the subsequent episodes went unanswered from VODO, though a total download count is available on the PioneerOne VODO page.

Using P2P (Peer to Peer) Methods to Distribute Film? **237**

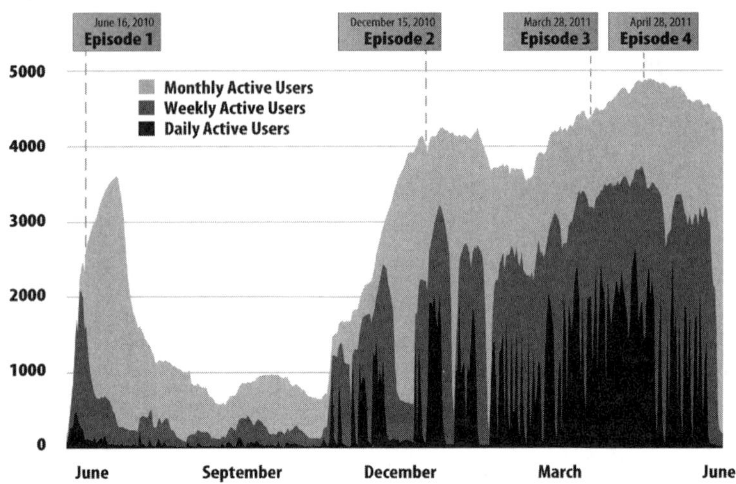

Activity on the PioneerOne *Facebook page over the course of the last year. Note how the fanbase builds and how much more activity has been happening with the release of each episode.*

The team has been selling t-shirts and posters through a website called Hackerthreads and has sold roughly $2000 worth of merchandise. However, given production and shipping costs, it has not been a good source of revenue. Once the season is completed, they plan to release all of the episodes on Netflix streaming and Amazon VOD.

Josh: *I think we've fared very well so far, though no one has made any money yet. We're putting the blood, sweat, and tears in now and making sacrifices in the hope that what we've started here will turn into something more robust and reliable in terms of profit. To be honest, the most valuable thing I think we got from the VODO distribution was the name recognition. Pioneer One is now a known commodity. It's a 'property' with value. I don't think we would have gotten that anywhere else.*

CASE STUDY SUMMARY

FILM TITLE/SHORT SYNOPSIS

Pioneer One is a sci-fi drama series about an investigation to find out the truth behind a mysterious cosmonaut who has fallen to earth.

OBJECTIVE OF THEIR RELEASE

There were many objectives to releasing the series for free using torrent sites and partnering with VODO to accomplish them. The creators wanted to reach as wide an audience as possible with very limited financial resources. They wanted to provide the VODO site with recurring content to attract and retain viewership, obviously a goal for both parties in the partnership. They wanted to fund the series' production through an ongoing crowd-funding initiative rather than going into personal debt or waiting for traditional financing. They wanted to create a valuable property that would be attractive to corporate sponsors and further the name recognition of the filmmakers within the industry.

APPROACH AND TOOLS TO REACH OBJECTIVE

The creators used the distribution power of the internet to reach a worldwide audience through the VODO network powered by BitTorrent while collecting donations from viewers and fans. Initially, the Kickstarter platform was used for the pilot episode, but the production now collects funds via VODO directly.

Episodes have been released sporadically over the last year, starting in June 2010. Episode 4 was released in April 2011.

The series has a Facebook presence, a Website with a constantly updated blog section and active comments from fans, a separate VODO page with Ustream vlog and donation widget for collecting payment, a Twitter account, YouTube and Vimeo channels, and a

Miso stream where fans can check in when watching episodes.

RESULTS

The project has raised $64,975 [as of May 3] on the VODO platform for production expenses and over $70,000 in total including the early Kickstarter funding. Four episodes have been released with another 2 planned for this season, and production is in progress for episode 5. Total downloads of the series number 3,037,271. The project won an award for "Best Drama Pilot" at the 2010 New York Television Festival. No sponsorship money has been raised as of this writing.

P2P (PEER TO PEER) SITES ARE AN ASSET FOR FILM DISTRIBUTION: CASE STUDY OF *THE COSMONAUT*

The Cosmonaut, *directed by Nicolás Alcalá*
Photo courtesy of Ángel Trancón

The Cosmonaut (*El Cosmonauta*) is an upcoming Spanish science-fiction feature film written and directed by Nicolás Alcalá and produced by Carola Rodriguez and Bruno Teixidor. It is the first feature-length project of Riot Cinema Collective and is notable for its use of crowd-funding, Creative Commons license (CC BY NC), crowd-sourcing and using P2P file sharing in its distribution to audiences.[11]

The project was one of the first in Spain to use crowd-funding during the development of the project. This resulted in massive press coverage within Spain, which soon spread to the world. Riot Cinema Collective did not use any third party crowd-funding sites like Kickstarter or Indiegogo because at the time, international projects were not eligible. Contributions continue to be accepted through a PayPal account or via text message.

> **Nicolás Alcalá:** *We launched our campaign site and we showed up in two of the most-read blogs in Spain, and from there it jumped to coverage on every blog in Spain and then to traditional media, and we were covered in probably every media outlet in Spain. I don't know if it was because people were excited about the project, or we were the first to do this or a mix of both.*

Regardless, it helped them to raise over 37,000€ for the project. Unlike most crowd-funding efforts, participants contributed by buying items from a special store which can be found on *The Cosmonaut* website rather than receiving "perks."

The communications team, a mix of volunteers and professional publicists who are working on a deferred basis, pitched the news story to influential publications. To date, news stories about the project have appeared in more than 400 media publications

---

11   "The Cosmonaut," *Wikipedia.* (http://www.sellingyourfilm.com/P2P-32.html)

and blogs. Nicolás credits the success of the ongoing campaign to having a professional website and an intriguing pitch video, as well as continuous social media efforts. The campaign started in May 2009. "I think it was also the way it was presented; for only 2 Euros you were buying into a project, not just giving charity," said Jennifer Warren, a consultant on the project. The 2 Euros gets a participant's name in closing credits, a producer's certificate, and a badge with the project's bird logo on it.

> **Nicolás:** *There were many people who bought badges from the store and they wore them around and recognized someone else who was wearing one too, so they said it felt like they belonged to the same group, even when they didn't yet know each other.*

It was a very smart tactic for building community around a film! So far they have made a net profit of 24,000€ from merchandise, mainly t-shirts.

For the past 2 years, the team has been committed to building up audience engagement and community. This is happening before even one frame of the project has been shot.

> **Nicolás:** *We decided early on not to be on every online platform, just being simple and choosing a few. We chose to have our blog, a Facebook page, a Twitter account, a Flickr account and a Vimeo account.*

The blog content is devoted to regularly updating the audience on what is happening with the production as well as personal thoughts and perspectives from the filmmaking team.

> **Nicolás:** *We talk about everything related to the movie, about collaborations with other people. We also talk about space, indie filmmaking, creative commons issues, and our views on piracy issues. It is a place you can come and learn*

about us as people, what we believe and what we are doing related to the movie; sometimes silly stuff like a picture of someone asleep at their desk while working on the project's development. We just make it more personal and allow people to feel like they are inside the workings of the production. We find that people respond the most when you tell personal stories.

These stories help build a real connection, a real relationship with the filmmaking team that can last well beyond this project.

The filmmaking team interacts with fans both online and offline. Here is a Cosmonaut flashmob in Spain conducted with the film's fans. Each fan was asked to cover himself in aluminum foil "space suits."
Photo courtesy of Daniel Torrelló

Nicolás: *We have found over the last few years that we are telling two stories through our blog. One is about the story of* The Cosmonaut *and the other is about young filmmakers trying to make a movie and we have put a lot of effort into both of them. I am the screenwriter of the project and I* *want to touch people with the story of* The Cosmonaut, *get them to feel something, and solicit feedback. But in sharing the story of all of us working on the project, we also want the feedback and fans to feel empathy with us as young filmmakers through our process. I don't think people will ever get bored of hearing about a very human story too.*

The team is also very active on Twitter, often posting relevant links to news stories of interest to their audience and carrying on conversations.

Nicolás: *The whole team uses the account and posts several times a day. When we were close to the 1,000th producer, we announced that over Twitter.*

In offering advice on building up a community, Nicolás admits that it takes a lot of time and effort, while feedback on the content can be unpredictable.

Nicolás: *It is very frustrating when you put out content and no one reacts! You can put content on Facebook you think will rock and zero comments come back. And you post something that is pretty insignificant, and it gets 50 comments. You just can't easily predict, you just have to test different things, different times of day.*

Riot Cinema is also quite committed to working in collaboration with their audience. They held a competition for the community to take 41 scenes from the initial film trailer and remix them into something new. The winner of the competition was Robert Pratten from Zen Films, chosen from over 100 submissions. They partnered with the Lomography Society to hold a photo contest where participants could win camera packs. It resulted in over 200 hundred photo submissions.

Nicolás: *We think we won't lose anything by having our*

The team was meticulous about formulating their business
plan, which takes elements from the traditional film business (investment, licensing, some territorial and format rights), and mixes
them with audience collaboration and engagement, experimental
distribution methods and conceiving alternate revenue streams. It
explains that the project will use existing online tools for audience
engagement and content collaboration from the beginning. Those
elements go way beyond the amount of interactivity normally
expected by a film's audience and help set the project apart from
most efforts in the film world because they foster close audience
relationships rather than dependence on mass advertising.

Nicolás: *From the beginning, we spent a lot of time on this
plan. We have a plan on how to release it, how to get revenues from it, how to communicate that to brands and busi-
nesses. We want to make a mix of the traditional model and
a new one. I think that is why we have received attention
so far.*

With the media coverage of their crowd-funding effort as well as their business plan, opportunities for speaking at conferences such as Power to the Pixel in London and TedxMadrid in Spain soon followed, along with the chance to pitch the project to funding bodies, investors and brands.

> **Nicolás:** *We are not highly skilled professionals who devote all our time to seeking out speaking opportunities. We just communicate with people the way we would like to be spoken with, it is very natural for all of us.*

He credits these early opportunities with sharpening the plan's focus because each investor, film funding body or corporate brand they met with challenged them with questions.

Leon Ockenden is Stas, the lost cosmonaut
Photo courtesy of Daniel Mayrit

The project's release plan consists of a day-and-date release online to file sharing sites, which will be the free version of the film;

VOD for subscription services (Netflix, LoveFilm etc.), iTunes download for easy viewing on tablets/iPhone, DVD available from their site and brick and mortar stores, (at present there is a distributor in place for Spain), and theatrically via live event screenings around the world. They also plan to license the film for broadcast. Their revenue streams will include the iTunes download, the DVD sales, VOD/broadcast licensing, brand sponsorship and pricing for the transmedia elements, as well as continued sales of merchandise items from the official *Cosmonaut* store.

The team anticipates the creation of a steady stream of content during production to be used for keeping audiences interested in the production process via their blog and social media work, but also for transmedia elements, which will have a free component and a paid component.

> **Nicolás:** *We will have an app [mobile phone application] with a game that will probably be free up to a certain level and then a paid option beyond that. We will release a novel version, of which the first 3 chapters will be free and then to finish the story, you will pay for the rest. Part of the transmedia storytelling is listening to calls between the characters. We are talking to technology companies and brands that might want to integrate with this content.*

There is also revenue in licensing derivative works for commercial purposes. While Creative Commons licenses cover remixing and sharing content from the production footage, they prohibit use of the material for financial gain. For anyone who wishes to use material from the project in order to profit financially, a license will have to be arranged with Riot Cinema Collective.

> **Nicolás:** *As an example, a guy with a music company in Berlin called us and said he loved the project and asked all of his musicians to write a song inspired by the movie that he wants to sell. We are working with him to design the packag-*

The budget for the project is set at 860,000€. Besides the crowd-funded development money, part of the budget is paid with co-production funding coming from a partnership with Phenomena Films, *who has made a significant investment of money as well as production services in Russia and Latvia.* In return, 29% of the project's rights and future profits will go to Phenomena. Another 169,086€ has been raised through private investors (450 of them!) and the team has been awarded a 100,000€ grant from the Cinematography Institute of Spain to develop the transmedia elements of the project. The team also received an innovation award of 8,000€ from National Television in Spain, and a 3,000€ entrepreneurship award from the European Union given by the group Campus Party.

One week before shooting was to begin on the project in May, the crew was told that one of their investors would have to pull some of the financing, leaving them with a 40,000€ shortfall. In a panic, the crew recorded a video appeal to their supporters asking for help to make up the deficit within 30 days. Within 72 hours, the community put together over 60,000€ in contributions from 278 donors, thus saving the production. Two weeks later the total amount raised was 130.000€, a number that keeps growing although the campaign has already finished. This is a testament to the power of their audience of fans and companies who believe in their work. The film is now in production throughout the summer of 2011.

So far, the filmmakers have secured DVD distribution in Spain through Cameo. The online distribution will utilize Mubi.com, Indieflix and VODO, and there is a VOD agreement with rtve.es. As the production is completed, it is likely that many more territories and format licenses will be sold. Imagina International Sales is the agency that will be handling sales for international territories once the project is completed. From *The Cosmonaut* site, 143 DVDs have been pre-ordered by fans.

Max Wrottesley as Andrei and Katrine de Candole as Yulia, part
of the love triangle story of The Cosmonaut
Photo courtesy of Daniel Mayrit

While online distribution will make up the bulk of the release, *The Cosmonaut* will have some live event theatrical screenings.

> **Nicolás:** *How big this strategy will be depends on the kinds of deals we are able to close. Our idea is to close deals with local distributors in different territories who are willing to work with our strategy, which is based on a demand-it model where the audience puts in requests for local screenings. The basic idea is to create an experience, to make it something unique, not replicable. We want to have interaction*

with mobile devices where the last episode of the web series we are creating [part of the transmedia work] is released during the month prior to the premiere of the film and leads the audience right into the first scene of the theatrical film. We want to have parties thrown for those attending the theatrical with "Cosmonaut Cocktails" featuring product from, say, an alcohol sponsor, live VJs remixing images of the film [à la Peter Greenaway with Tulse Luper Suitcases], live Q&A with the cast and crew, a display of costumes and props from the production, merchandising, and so on. Going to the theater to see the film will be an experience you will want to share with your friends. That's why we think people will decide to pay to attend even though they have the film for free on the internet.

The Cosmonaut began production in Latvia in late May, and no doubt their progress can be followed on their blog or social media pages.

CASE STUDY SUMMARY

FILM TITLE/SHORT SYNOPSIS

The Cosmonaut is a multi-faceted project consisting of a feature film, mobile applications, a novel and web series all centered around the story of a cosmonaut, Stas Arsenievich, whose spaceship runs off course during a mission. His friends at mission control spend 7 months searching for it to no avail. When the spaceship reappears on Earth, Stas is nowhere to be found, even though a series of eerie radio transmissions supposedly broadcast by Stas claim that he has actually come back home and that he found the Earth completely empty.

OBJECTIVE OF THEIR RELEASE

There are many objectives the filmmakers are trying to accomplish. The company wants to show how films distributed for free via the internet can also make money. They also want to build a name for themselves within the industry that can be used to attract more investment in their work and further opportunities. Retaining control over how their work is made, marketed and distributed is also a goal as well as direct communication with an audience that is interested in their style of storytelling.

APPROACH AND TOOLS TO REACH OBJECTIVE

Funded by a mixture of crowd-funding, outside investment, grant funding and sponsorship, this is the first transmedia property created in Spain and the first to introduce the concept of crowd-funding in that country. Distribution will consist of using P2P networks, theatrical live events, traditional DVD, broadcast and foreign rights sales, selling DVDs from the film's site and selling non-exclusive SVOD and VOD broadcast rights. Some traditional DVD rights have beenpresold and they will seek to sell more internationally.

The creators have been building an audience for their work over the past 2 years largely using a blog on their website, regular posts and updates on their Facebook and Twitter accounts, a collection of photographs of the creators, cast, crew, locations, preproduction process and on set photography on the project's Flickr page and via Livestream. They are recording regular video blog updates and posting them to their Vimeo page.

They have partnered with organizations like Lomography Society and Mubi.com to offer contests that benefit the project (in content submissions) and raise awareness for the organizations.

RESULTS

The project has raised over almost 300,000€ from private investors, 24,000€ from merchandise and received grants and cash awards totaling 110,000€. The filmmakers have secured DVD distribution in Spain through Cameo, pre-sale via a co-production agreement with Phenomena Films in Latvia and Russia, digital distribution via VODO, MUBI and Indieflix, (which will enable access to Amazon VOD, iTunes and Netflix), and broadcast VOD agreement through rtv.es. All of this was accomplished before one frame of the film was shot. Film is now in production in Latvia/Russia. The project has won the INVI Award for Audio Visual Innovation.

MAKING MONEY BY SETTING YOUR CONTENT FREE: CASE STUDY OF *SITA SINGS THE BLUES*

Sita Sings the Blues, *an animated feature by Nina Paley.*

By now, I am sure you are wondering how you will sustain your-self as an artist by giving away your content for free. You would not be the first to ask this; industry executives all moan about how they cannot compete with free. Their interim solution is to issue take-down notices and bring lawsuits to file sharers. Nina Paley, an independent animator, teacher and cartoonist had a better idea. She has built a revenue generating business by selling scarce goods to compliment her film, *Sita Sings the Blues*, which is available for free worldwide on the internet. She did not start out with this kind of business model in mind; it took a run-in with copyright law to make her reinvent the film distribution model.

Sita was the product of Nina's marital break-up. Having lived in India during the marriage, she was exposed to the culture and stories. When she settled in Brooklyn, a rereading of the Rama-yana, (an ancient Sanskrit tale considered one of the main texts of the Hindu religion), and a fascination with the music of the 1920s, (particularly that of jazz singer Annette Hanshaw), inspired her to tell the tale of Sita, wife of Prince Rama, as a parallel to her own life. The creation is an amazing mix of animation styles, color, humor, human emotion and music. It was in using Han-shaw's music that Nina ran up against the dilemma of many inde-pendent filmmakers; paying for music licensing or changing the soundtrack. While Hanshaw's recorded music was in the public domain, the compositions (lyrics, notation etc.) are still protected under copyright laws due to retroactive copyright term extensions by Congress. When attempting to clear the copyright restrictions, Nina was given the runaround for months by every rights-holder she tried to contact, finally hiring a law firm to act as intermedi-ary. After being required to pay $500 per song to even talk to the rights-holders, she was told she would have to pay various music licensing services over $220,000 to show the film legally outside of film festivals. Without those music clearances there was no hope of finding distribution or even giving the film away for free, but the cost for the clearances was more than the total budget of the film, and no distributor wanted to take on that cost to secure the rights. Nina eventually signed a "step deal" through a rights clearance house to pay $50,000, taking out a loan to pay the cost. The film is now able to be distributed legally, although there is a nearly $2 per disc fee payable to the licensing services for each sale. A total fee breakdown explaining the charges is available on the film's website.

Chicago Sun-Times film critic Roger Ebert said of Sita Sings the Blues, *"I am enchanted. I am swept away. I am smiling from one end of the film to the other. It is astonishingly original."*

THE FIGHT FOR FREE CULTURE

The whole experience left Nina questioning the use of copyright law, intellectual property "protections" and its detrimental effect on artistic freedom and innovation. While the songs were integral to her work's thesis and could not be replaced, (Nina has said the songs provided an authenticity to show how the stories in the Ramayana transcend time, culture and experience), they were largely forgotten by modern audiences. Her use of them should have been viewed as breathing new life into neglected property. Instead of capitalizing on the renewed attention, licensors prefer to hold the artists wanting to revitalize them for ransom. It also made her an activist for the Free Culture movement, a social movement promoting the freedom to modify creative works in the form of free content and distribute them by using the internet.[12] Many artists are not in agreement yet with the goals of the free culture movement and cannot see how allowing their content to be freely distributed, modified, built upon and used by others for profit would be at all beneficial. Nina explains her position on this:

> **Nina Paley:** *I understand this is a totally different mindset than we have been trained to believe. If you use the premise that people will not pay for content that they can get for free, then it does not even matter if other people are making money from it or not. If people are getting something for free that you think they would have paid for, it leads you to think that they have stolen it from you.*

Creative Commons licensing, previously discussed in this chapter, is used by free culturists, but there are only 2 of the 6 license categories that are actually considered to fit within the terms of the society (CC BY and CC BY-SA).

> **Nina:** *People making free culture projects cannot use a CC NC (non commercial) license, even if they get special permission to use the work in a commercial way because*

---

12 "Free Culture Movement," *Wikipedia.* (http://www.sellingyourfilm.com/P2P-52.html)

The principles of Free Culture do not restrict the ability to profit from selling one's work; they restrict the ability to have a monopoly on the work. Nina has been asked if she feared a large corporation like Disney might take her work and profit from it, because legally, under her licensing terms they do not have to pay her any money.

Nina: *I don't fear it because it would mean that for the first time Disney would be releasing something that cannot be restricted; they could not keep anyone else from using that work too and I would consider that a win. But they aren't going to do this. It would set a precedent against their current business model, which is structured to lock down content and severely restrict the access to it. Any entity can do whatever they want with my content, even profit from it, as long as their business model isn't dependent on restricting others from doing the same.*

HITTING THE FESTIVAL CIRCUIT AND NOT FINDING DISTRIBUTION DEALS

Sita Sings the Blues made its world debut at the Berlin International Film Festival (Berlinale) in February 2008. As this was Nina's first film, she was unsure of the procedure for introducing a film to the marketplace.

Nina: *When I first started all of this, I knew nothing and I just did what everyone said you are supposed to do. When I was selected for the Berlinale, everyone said I needed a sales rep.*

Nina signed with attorney Steven Beers. She paid him $5,000 in upfront fees and agreed to a 10% commission. She did not hire a publicist and noted that attendance at her screenings in Berlin was quite poor. Winning an award, Special Mention Gen-14+ definitely helped raise awareness both at the festival and in the aftermath.

At the time, Nina had not yet cleared the music for the film, which presented a problem for Beers in attracting sales offers. All of the larger distribution houses passed on the film and the only offers that came were proposing upfront payments in the $10,000-$20,000 range for all rights during a minimum 10 year period. She was also told that the most she could realistically hope for in net sales on the film was $25,000, possibly $50,000 if the team was particularly successful. For a film that would eventually cost $270,000 when the loan for the music licensing was included, this did not seem like a good deal to Nina. She passed on the offers.

Rama, Hanuman and Sita singing in the rain

After less than a year on the festival circuit that included official selections at Tribeca, Ottawa, Seattle International and Melbourne, which included winning awards (to date 35), Nina decided the conventional way of releasing her film was not to be. She made a commitment to free culture, and though she continued to try for distribution deals, few wanted to take on the film.

> **Nina:** *I remember talking to one pretty well-respected distributor and asked if they were willing to service this in theaters and release the DVD, but that they wouldn't have a monopoly on it because it would be "copyleft." They said "Absolutely not."*

Nina said to Beers' credit he was very open-minded about her decision and wished her well.

THEATRICAL SCREENINGS

Eventually Nina found 2 theatrical distributors, GKids and Shadow Distribution, who agreed to take on the film under the Share Alike terms. GKids fulfilled theater commitments east of the Mississippi, Shadow west of it. In total, the film grossed $81,674 over a two year period. In addition to theatrically booked screenings, the film has continued to play festivals and privately organized screenings in cities worldwide, garnering self-motivated donations to Nina, which she collects on the film's website.

> **Nina:** *No one has to tell me if they are having a screening and no one has to say why they are sending a donation, though some people do. So I don't know how many times the film has screened truthfully.*

Nina knows that the film played in New York for 5 weeks at the IFC Center in Greenwich Village and a couple of weekends at Symphony Space on the Upper West Side. It also played at Chicago's Gene Siskel Film Center, ran for 1 week at the Laemmle Music Hall in Los Angeles, and showed at San Francisco's Red Vic. From February 2008 to February 2011, it is known to have screened 247 times. Despite the film's availability online, people still want to see it in a theater.

> **Nina:** *In New York, people would come up to me afterward and say "I love your film, I've watched it 3 times online," and they just bought a ticket to see it in a theater. Seeing it online made them buy that ticket.*

SELLING DVD COPIES

Nina found a DVD distributor in FilmKaravan, who distributes and makes deals with other distributors like IndiePix to sell DVDs. These are all non-exclusive deals; anyone can distribute DVDs of her work. She said she hasn't received a statement from FilmKaravan in ages, but in the beginning they were selling quite aggressively. Most of her DVD sales come from her e-store.

With regard to how you make money from work freely available, listen up. To date, Nina herself has sold 3,134 standard edition DVDs and collected $62,680; 102 PAL version DVDs grossed $2220 (she splits the gross 50/50 on these sales with Question-Copyright.org who host her store); 164 artist edition DVDs, which are signed and numbered and cost $100, grossed $16,400. For the artist editions she earns 100% of the gross, though with all of the copies she must hold back the $2 per disc license levy. The thought of making DVD copies did not occur to her when she initially released the film on archive.org.

> **Nina:** *Much to my surprise, people started telling me they wanted to buy DVDs. So with that pressure, I scrambled to get them produced. I never thought, and most people would tell you this, that people would buy a film that was available for free. It took 2 months to produce those DVDs and I'm doing okay with that now. I would still do everything the same, I still would have released for free first and it is still*

Using P2P (Peer to Peer) Methods to Distribute Film? **259**

MERCHANDISE SALES

In addition to selling copies, Nina also created a wealth of merchandise. There are t-shirts, posters, stickers, pendants, pins, stuffed sculptures etc., all with characters and motifs from the film. In total, the e-store has grossed $146,470 to date (June 2011). Remember, a distributor told her the most she could hope to net was $50,000, and that would only happen if they were extremely successful.

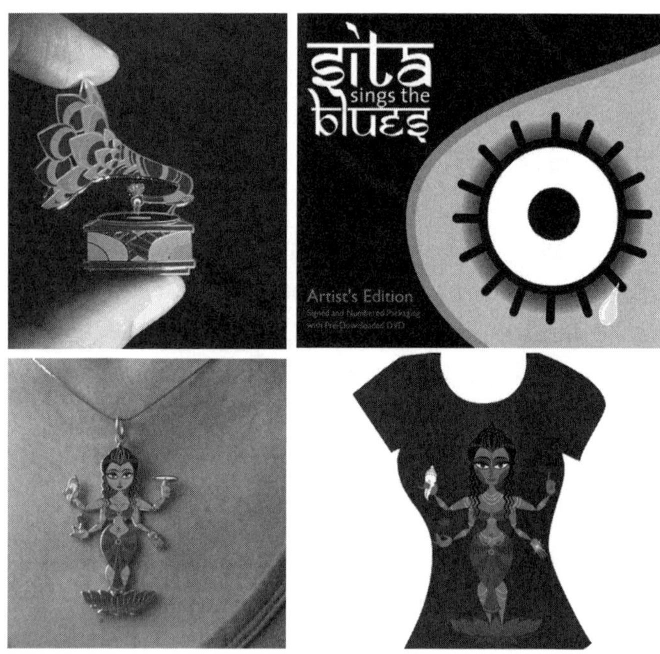

Merchandise from the film includes high quality pins, tshirts and necklaces as well as artist signed DVD copies (yes, from a film you can watch for free online!)

She is also working on quilting patterns, which will be open-sourced.

> **Nina:** *The quilts are not part of the merchandise; they take about 200 hours each to make and if I sold them, I would want $20,000. I don't think the market exists yet. My theory is, since they are an original work of art, the value increases the more copies of it are circulating. So my plan is to get as many copies, even if it is only photographs and patterns, to circulate and drive up the demand of the originals that I did and then I could sell those quilts. The patterns are all my original design. I also have reserved the domain name opensourcequilts.com, so when I have more, I will release all of the patterns on the site and anyone can use them, share them and ask people to copy them as much as possible. Copying quilts is a lot of work, but I hope some people will do it.*

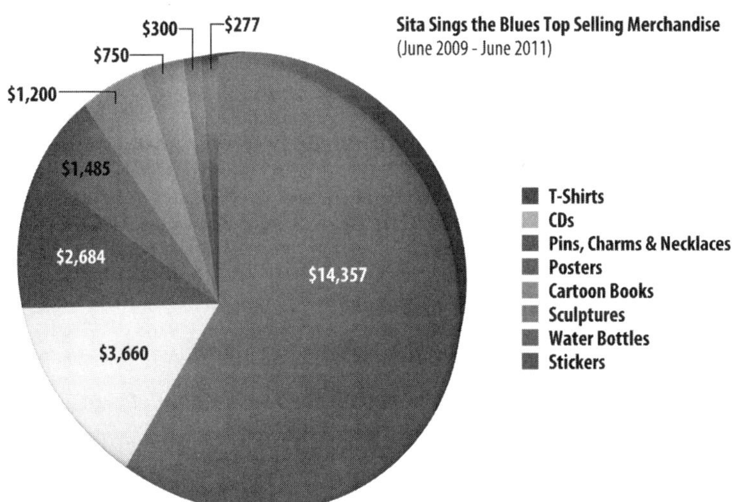

This chart reflects the top 10 best selling merchandise items through Nina Paley's eStore from June 2009-June 2011

TV AND CABLE SALES?

WNET Channel 13 in New York City, a public broadcast station, has shown *Sita* in the US. TV sales for free culture properties remain difficult to achieve, mainly because of the legal hassles endemic to broadcast stations.

> **Nina:** *Broadcasters all have legal departments and they want permission; they think the only way you can show something is if you have the right to do it and they want to negotiate for those rights. When I am approached by stations asking for rights I say, "Well, you already have the right, show it, but if you want to negotiate my endorsement, let's talk about that." It is such a weird concept for them that they just give up. That's the worst part of this free culture initiative. Free culture is indigestible to legal departments. They don't understand that procedure so they determine it is too much trouble and give up.*

Channel 13 approached Nina when a lawyer working there came across her blog and contacted her. Australian Public Broadcasting and LinkTV have also shown the film. "Anybody can show it and I wish they would. It is very frustrating." Together she has collected only $4,000 from these sources.

IPHONE AND ANDROID APPS

Both have been developed without Nina's involvement. Some are free and some cost $3.99 because the developer/distributor must pay the $2 licensing levy on each download. If the charge were only $.99, it would cost the developer more money than she is making.

> **Nina:** *That levy has done nothing but solidify my commitment to free culture. It is better to just give them away as free*

promotion copies [she only pays the levy on copies sold].
*So thanks, crazy, extortionate, corporate entities. I have still
benefitted even when you don't get money from my work.*

MARKETING, PROMOTION, AUDIENCE BUILDING

Aside from making a film print for Berlin, which cost $30,000 and was paid for through donations and good faith interest-free loans from her blog readers, Nina has paid almost nothing to promote the film. "It has all been done by the audience. I gave the film to the audience and the audience took it and promoted the hell out of it. The fact that it was in film festivals really helped that; it was great. People definitely heard about it from other people."

It took 3 years to make the film, and Nina blogged about it the whole time. Starting in 2005, pre-YouTube, she put up Quicktime videos when she was finished with sections to get feedback.

> **Nina:** *I remember the day that someone else wrote about my blog because before that, it was really just friends reading it. Then* Boing Boing *picked up that story and then my blog stopped working because of the traffic to it.*

Word spread many years before the film was ready for release, and people continually checked Nina's blog to see what was happening.

> **Nina:** *I am still surprised anyone wants to read what I write on my blog. The whole story of the film's journey is surprising, delightful, amazing and wonderful. This* [audience building] *was all an accident; I don't feel like I did anything special, only what I naturally want to do which is share my work, what I am working on."*

Her blogging continues today.

She does have sympathy for those who do not want to share

their work experience through blogging.

> **Nina:** *I think the secret is that people shouldn't do things that are unnatural to them. If people really don't like to talk about what they do, if it is not comfortable for them, then I don't think the answer is for them to do that. There are other ways to connect with fans.*

She admits it is true that an artist must have fans, even a few, to start spreading the word. She also found that her readers were willing to help with advice and skills she didn't have.

> **Nina:** *They helped me take my large files and convert them to file sizes that they needed to spread it around. And they told me what they needed so I could produce it.*

She never outsources her voice to others for online communication.

> **Nina:** *When fans talk to me online it is really me. But it is a really addictive compulsion. My inability to pull myself away from the computer is an asset, at least in some way, but I have learned in the past year that I can't respond to every email. I used to answer every one immediately, but I get some hate mail and crazy stuff and students who want me to write their papers for them and tons of inquiries where the information they ask for is already online.*

Nina paid only two festival submission fees, Berlin and Chicago International, because she is from Illinois and wanted the film to play there. The rest of the festival screenings were by invitation, and a few paid screening fees to her. She made her biggest publicity push for the Tribeca Festival 2008, where she acted as the film's publicist.

> **Nina:** *I think I did write a press release, which is probably the most boring bit of literature known to man. For journal-*

OTHER REVENUE

As a free culture activist, Nina is invited to speak all over the world. Her ability to generate revenue from freely available content makes her a popular keynote speaker at colleges and conferences for which she is paid speaking fees that have brought in between $10,000-$15,000 in total income. She books these engagements herself, though she would love to be part of a speaker's bureau. "Through a bureau I could command higher rates. I hate to fly so I want the speaking dates to be worthwhile financially."

She also received $12,500 in prize money from film festivals and has received over $50,000 in donations from those who viewed her film for free. She did look for sponsorships and even left space in the film (the intermission section) to slot in branded content. She has yet to find any.

ORGANIZATIONAL OUTREACH

During production of the film, Nina submitted small chunks as short films to the Indo-American Arts Council film festival and various animation festivals, and held screenings with community arts organizations. Through her involvement with one in Brooklyn, she found her voice actors. She also found Indian journalists through these affiliations who wrote about what she was doing.

The film did not enjoy total acceptance within the Indian community, though. Hindu fundamentalists condemned her irreverence for their sacred text and hateful comments were left on her blog. Nina was taken aback by the condemnation, but believed that the open minded, cosmopolitan Indian community would understand her cross-cultural approach to the text. It seems that largely, they did. The film has screened many times in India, although it has no centralized distribution there.

DERIVATIVE WORK

Since Nina encourages others to remix, reinvent and build upon her work, there have been a few examples. There was a fashion line inspired by the film. "I wish they had just gone ahead and copied it rather than redrawing it, but it was quite a surprise for me." There are also music videos and remixes of the content.

CONCLUSION

Nina doesn't think her success would be attainable for every filmmaker.

> **Nina:** *It defies common wisdom for how these things work. I can't say that I knew this was how it would go, but by making it available for free to the fans, it has increased greatly in making the film successful.*

Also, it is a testament to the strength of the piece. In order for work to spread online, it must be exceptional and recognized as such. People don't share mediocre content; they don't recommend poorly produced content. If it doesn't touch someone enough to recommend it to someone else, it will not spread and you will not attract enough attention to lead to monetization in any meaningful way. Perhaps this is the real fear behind an artist or studios' hesitancy to set their content free. If they weren't forcing patrons to pay for content, would the viewers pay anyway?

CASE STUDY SUMMARY

FILM TITLE/SHORT SYNOPSIS

Sita Sings the Blues is an animated feature film retelling of the ancient Sanskrit tale of the Ramayana about Prince Rama and his wife Sita. The story is intertwined with real life events in the animator Nina Paley's life and is partially set to the music of 1920's jazz singer Annette Hanshaw.

OBJECTIVE OF THEIR RELEASE

The original objective was to seek traditional distribution through the use of a sales agent. When this did not occur, Nina decided to self-distribute the film under a copyleft/Share Alike license and put the film online for free. In this way she hoped the film would reach a wide audience with little cost and recoupment of the film's budget would happen through a variety of revenue streams.

Through her commitment to Free Culture, Nina wanted to serve as an example of how artists could create revenue-generating business models while distributing their work for free.

APPROACH AND TOOLS TO REACH OBJECTIVE

The film was put online at archive.org and YouTube, as well as many file sharing sites and was spread by its fans. The film was screened at hundreds of film festivals, as well as private screenings and in traditional cinemas. Revenue streams include merchandise, speaking engagements and distributor outlets. A partnership with the Questioncopyright.org organization provides for an e-store where merchandise is sold at a 50/50 gross split. The e-store is powered by Amplifier.

A fan base was built by continued maintenance of a personal blog and information about the film; its release pattern and any other facts are found on the film's dedicated website. There is a Facebook page, which is largely populated by fans without much maintenance by Nina.

The Share Alike license allows for anyone to distribute, remix, build upon and profit from this work. Attribution is required.

RESULTS

The film has netted over $150,000, which is much better than the original distributor's prediction of a $50,000 maximum. It is impossible to measure how many views and downloads the film has attracted (archive.org puts the download count at 339,724 from their site and YouTube's count is 476, 719 as of June 13, 2011) due to its free proliferation online, but at least 3416 DVD copies have been purchased.

The film has screened over 247 times throughout the world. As a result of her Free Culture activism, as well as her expertise as an animator and her engagement with the Ramayana, Nina is often paid to give lectures, which provides a source of income, raises her professional profile and contributes to awareness of the film.

List of Questions
Given to Participating Filmmakers

DISTRIBUTION SALES

1. Did you have a domestic sales rep? If so who?
2. What percentage do you owe them?
3. For how long?
4. Did you find them effective?
5. Do you have a foreign sales rep? If so who?
6. Did you find them effective?
7. What is your deal with them? (e.g. 25% plus expenses capped at $50,000)
8. How many consultants did you work with (name them)?
9. How effective were they?
10. How much did you spend on consultants?

LIVE EVENT THEATRICAL

FILM FESTIVALS

11. Did you premiere at a prominent festival?
12. How much did you spend to "open" at the festival—publicists etc.
13. Other than your Festival premiere, what was your strategy around Film Festivals in general? Did you play many or just a few, and why or why not?
14. Did you charge the Festivals screening fees to show your film? If so, how much did you gross?

15. Outside of the Festival circuit, did you hold community-based word-of-mouth/buzz screenings? Did you feel they were helpful? Do you have any way to empirically back that up?

CONVENTIONAL THEATRICAL

16. Did you do traditional theatrical and if so how long did you spend to set it up?
17. How much did you spend on the theatrical?
18. Did you use a service company?
19. If so which one?
20. How long was the theatrical run?
21. How many cities were full week runs?
22. How many cities were one-night events in traditional theatrical venues?
23. How much did you *gross* and *net*? Can you give a specific on your highest grossing week long run and lowest grossing week long run? Same for one-night events?

ALTERNATIVE THEATRICAL (INCLUDES NON, SEMI AND COMMUNITY THEATRICAL)

24. How many cities did you have alternative theatrical screenings?
25. If a separate number from conventional theatrical—how much did you spend to book your alternative theatrical release?
26. Did you attempt to monetize your community-based buzz screenings? If so, how did you do that (share of box office, rental fees paid by venues, etc)? Was this effort to monetize these screenings successful?
27. How much did you gross on your alternative theatrical release?

MERCHANDISE SALES

DVD SALES—VIA A DISTRIBUTOR

28.   How many DVD units did you sell via a distributor?
29.   How much did you receive from the DVD distributor? Are you still owed money?
30.   How many DVD units did you sell yourself?
31.   What did you gross?
32.   What are your terms with the distributor?
33.   If you buy your DVDs from your distributor—how much do you pay per unit?
34.   What has been your overall experience with your DVD distributor?

DVD AND OTHER MERCHANDISE SALES FROM YOUR WEBSITE OR AT EVENTS?

35.   What fulfillment company do you use? Or do you self fulfill?
36.   What has your experience been with your fulfillment company?
37.   How much have you made from your own DVD sales?
38.   How much have you made from other merchandise?

DIGITAL RIGHTS

TELEVISION AND CABLE

39.   Do you have a US TV deal? If so on what platform?
40.   How much did you make from the US TV Deal?
41.   Who made these sales?
42.   How many Cable VOD platforms are you on?
43.   Do you have a VOD aggregator – if so who?
44.   How much money have you made from VOD

"CONVENTIONAL" DIGITAL RIGHTS—(E.G. STREAMING, DOWNLOAD)

45.   What digital platforms is your film available on?

46.   How did it get onto them? Please be specific about which ones, length of time on etc.

47.   How many much money have you made via any and all digital distribution? If you can break it down by provider – please do (e.g. 10,000 iTunes, 7000 Hulu, etc)

48.   Any mobile App distribution? Please explain and go into detail if so.

FOREIGN SALES

49.   Any overall sales in outside the US— (e.g. all rights including theatrical, DVD, TV)

50.   Any Foreign TV sales only—and how much?

51.   If so please explain who handled, what deals were like and what the results have been.

PROMOTION AND SOCIAL MEDIA

52.   How much did you spend for the marketing and promotion of your release?

53.   How much did you spend on publicists? Please separate National, NY, LA, Regional, Affinity?

54.   Whom did you hire to help you with publicity?

55.   How much did you spend on social media? How many months? How much per month?

56.   Whom did you hire to help you with social media?

57.   Did you find your publicists or social media people effective?

58.   Did you track your online analytics related to specific promotional activities? (e.g. if you did a specific promotion did you track if your activity on your website, or other social media channels in-

creased and if so by how much?)

59. Did sales increase by any specific promotional activities? Can you be specific?
60. Did you purchase any media (print ads, radio or tv, web banner ads)? How much did you spend on each?
61. Were the media buys effective?
62. Did you purchase Facebook Ads or Google Ads? How much did you spend? Were they effective?
63. Any YouTube stats? Please explain and go into detail if so. What activity led to more views?
64. Did you do any online competitions? If so can you go into detail—were they effective?
65. Did you push any other form of content on the web (e.g. video content)? How did you do this? Did you pay for this? Did it help your statistics—#s or $s?
66. Did you do any other kind of media for email, like, share promotion? If so was it effective?

ORGANIZATIONAL OUTREACH

67. Did you enlist the help of Grassroots Organizations to help promote your film? If so, did they promote the Festival screenings, the theatrical screenings, the DVD release, the Digital Platforms…or what? Do you think their promotion was successful for your bottom line?
68. Did you develop financial relationships with Grassroots Organizations to either sponsor the film or help you monetize event screenings? If so, was this effort successful?
69. What were your primary challenges in terms of getting grassroots buzz, and what do you think you could have done better?

OTHER MONEY QUESTIONS

70.   Did you raise money for the distribution? If so how much?
71.   How did you raise money for distribution?
72.   How did that affect the revenue stream—other investors—$ waterfall?
73.   How much of the budget was equity investment (to be paid back)?
74.   How much money in the budget was from grants, sponsorship, bartering? Please explain
75.   Regarding investors: who invested what?
76.   What were the backend deals?
77.   Have investors been paid back?
78.   Have the below the line crew been paid? Assuming yes, just at production or was there any backend participation?
79.   Have the director and cast been paid? Please go into specifics.
80.   Any prize money?
81.   Remake rights sales? Any other deals that came out of the film's exhibition?
82.   Any automated distribution?

About the Authors

THE FILM COLLABORATIVE

ORLY RAVID, FOUNDER/CO-EXECUTIVE DIRECTOR AND JEFFREY WINTER, CO-EXECUTIVE DIRECTOR

The Film Collaborative (TFC) is the first non-profit organization devoted to film distribution-education and full-service distribution of independent cinema. Since its launch at Sundance 2010, TFC has become a trusted and sought after brand in the filmmaking community. TFC has facilitated distribution worldwide and has worked with over 100 films (in just over a year), many of which are official selections at festival such as Sundance, Cannes, SXSW, Berlinale, Toronto International Film Festival, New Directors/New Films, Los Angeles Film Festival and AFI FEST. TFC has a Foreign Language Oscar™ Initiative with Palm Springs International Film Festival and is invited to speak at festivals worldwide on a monthly basis, particularly on hybrid and new media distribution. Additional initiatives of The Film Collaborative include its suite of online resource tools for filmmakers (distripedia™), its Global Shorts Initiative, which recently kicked off with the release of a "Best Gay & Lesbian Shorts" collection under its FestSelects™ brand on a variety of digital platforms, including a YouTube rental channel in the U.S. and an iPhone App available in 90 countries. TFC has been asked to provide educational services to uniFrance and has advised Sundance on its new Artists Services initiative.

For more information about TFC please go to thefilmcollaborative.org.
Facebook: facebook.com/thefilmcollaborative
Twitter: twitter.com/filmcollab
YouTube: youtube.com/thefilmcollaborative

JON REISS

Named one of "10 Digital Directors to Watch" by *Daily Variety*, Jon Reiss is a critically acclaimed filmmaker whose experience releasing his most recent documentary feature, Bomb It with a hybrid strategy was the inspiration for writing Think Outside the Box Office: The Ultimate Guide to Film Distribution in the Digital Era, the first step-by-step guide for filmmakers to distribute and market their films. In that book he created the concept of the Producer of Marketing and Distribution (PMD) in order create a new crew member who would be in charge of a film's release.

As a consultant, Reiss is unique as one of the only filmmakers who works with other filmmakers throughout the world helping them devise strategies to release their films. He and Sheri Candler also train and supervise PMDs working on individual films.

Reiss has worked with IFP, the Sundance Institute, Screen Australia, Film Independent, Creative Scotland, The South Australian Film Corporation and numerous film schools and festivals to devise ways to educate and help independent filmmakers in the new economic landscape. He has conducted over a dozen TOTBO Workshops over three continents in the last year and is the year round distribution and marketing mentor at the IFP Filmmaker Labs. He also teaches in the Film Directing Program at Cal Arts.

Reiss is working on two more book projects: the first is devoted to the PMD, the second book takes the structure of distribution and marketing outlined in TOTBO and applies it to all art forms and media; music, dance, theater, art, photography, book publishing/authorship, comedy, etc.

For more information about Jon Reiss go to: jonreiss.com
Facebook: facebook.com/reiss.jon
Twitter: twitter.com/jon_reiss
Jon is also on Google+, add him to your circles

SHERI CANDLER

Sheri Candler is an inbound marketing strategist who helps independent filmmakers build identities for themselves and their films. Through the use of online tools such as social networking, podcasts, blogs, organizational outreach, online media publications, and radio, she assists filmmakers in building an engaged and robust online community for their work that can be used to monetize effectively. She has participated in panels and workshops on social media marketing for filmmakers at the American Film Market, Los Angeles Latino International Film Festival, National Screen Institute of Canada and National Association of Latino Independent Producers. She writes articles for Microfilmmaker Magazine covering the issues of marketing and distribution for microbudget films and is the co founder of Twitter discussion series #filmin140, a monthly virtual panel covering topics of interest to the independent filmmaker.

For more information about Sheri Candler go to: shericandler.com
Facebook: www.facebook.com/SheriCandlerMarketingandPublicity
Twitter: twitter.com/shericandler
Sheri is also on Google+, add her to your circles

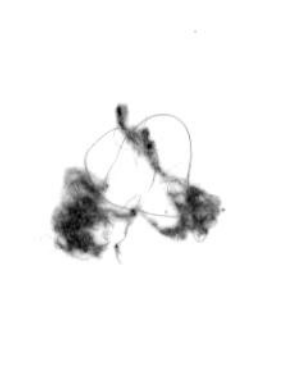